scream

scream

A MEMOIR OF GLAMOUR AND DYSFUNCTION

tama janowitz

DEY ST.

An Imprint of WILLIAM MORROW

DEY ST.

Photographs, unless otherwise credited, are provided courtesy of the author.

Photograph on page 279: Arlene Studio for the *Smith Alumnae Quarterly*. Used by permission.

Photograph on page 281: © Marvel. Used by permission.

This is a memoir. *My* memories. It is what *I* remember. Except some of the people were a lot worse. I changed some names and minor details. Quotes are re-created to the best of my ability based on my keen recollection of the events.

HarperCollins books may be purchased for educational, business, or sales promotional use. For information, please e-mail the Special Markets Department at SPsales@harpercollins.com.

FIRST EDITION

Designed by Suet Yee Chong

Library of Congress Cataloging-in-Publication Data has been applied for.

ISBN 978-0-06-239132-2

16 17 18 19 20 RRD 10 9 8 7 6 5 4 3 2 1

For John Laughlin

SLIP

by Phyllis Janowitz (1930–2014)

My mother blew away in a molecular
diffusion. I never stopped asking her
questions although her answers
could not be heard over weather conditions.
Something remains: a smile, an obsolete refrain.

I remember my mother in Queens; in New Jersey;
in Portugal; Lima; Franconia, New Hampshire.
Clever woman, she is liquid mercury
between my fingers. I see her or touch her
but there is no holding her, not her arms,

not her hair. The little that is leftover
will presently roll out of reach.
As for me, I will continue the family tradition,
vanishing, one part then another
with the argyle socks on the line

cotton sheets and underwear piecemeal
swept off in an easterly direction
the same way I saw her come towards me
when the Amherst bus stopped at Leverett Station
setting her down in a blizzard—she

staggered, hip-deep in snow
rigid cold stiffening her connections
to a house she had never been to,
finding the right road regardless—
or when suitcase open, her torn

umbrella turning inside out, she flung
herself from a taxicab in Boston
at midnight, the wind baneful
and Commonwealth Avenue too chilly to welcome
a visitor so temporary, so uncontainable.

scream

a visit to dad

I have decided to leave you my property." It's my father on the phone. "Please come at once."

Dad has lived for fifty-five years in western Massachusetts, five or six hours away from where I'm living in upstate New York. I moved here to look after my mom, and my daughter, Willow, who is seventeen, left Brooklyn to move in with me. Then, I had to put Mom in the home. Now it's just me and Willow. My husband, Tim, still lives in Brooklyn, but he'll meet us in Albany and make the trip with us.

We take my mom's car, a 1995 Mazda: it only has twenty-five thousand miles on it, but it is still a very old car. I have had the wheels replaced, the cooling system, but it seems every time I drive it, it needs a valve replacement or some other bypass operation.

My father owns two hundred acres of swampland. It's mortgaged up to the hilt. It's got a mortgage, a reverse mortgage, and restrictions. Still, it's a beautiful swamp.

Dad has summoned me to discuss how I will handle my inheritance.

In particular, he doesn't want my dogs in his house, although he used to have a dog. I guess he means after he dies. Before, when I visited, I had to stay in a motel. Now he says he will cover the floor of the guest room with plastic if I will come to visit, and that I can bring the poodles.

By the time we arrive it's evening.

My father greets us at the front door. He is dancing with excitement. "Hi! Welcome! Sooooo . . . my drug dealer is coming over in a little while!"

He's a pothead. Dad is eighty-three years old and has smoked marijuana every day since I was eight. That's almost fifty years—not quite, but let's round it up. And when I say "every day," what I mean is he smokes *all* day. From when he gets up until just before bedtime, every couple of hours. When he started, he smoked joints and the pot wasn't so powerful. Now the stuff is so strong that when his friends come over and he offers a bowl, bad things happen. They fall over in a faint, they go backward in a chair and smash their heads on the tile floor, they fall into the swamp, they get in car accidents.

"My friend Alan took one puff and had a seizure!" he said once, laughing. Dad barely gets high from it, that's how accustomed to it he is.

He starts the day with a "public smoke" in his garden room (the one with the hot tub and the orchids). Or at the kitchen table, or on one of the many screened decks overlooking the swamp. Maybe three times a day it's a public smoke. Then two or three times a day he goes up to his room for a private toke—you can smell it as the smoke plumes out under his bedroom door, great wafts of it, gusts of it, like a skunk got in the house, which is what I always think at first until I realize, Oh, that's just Daddy!

There is not an hour when Dad is not stoned. Still, it's not enough.

I can tell when Dad needs another few puffs because . . . well, he starts to decline. The black cloud of rage and hate comes over him and he gets angrier and blacker and bleaker. Then he has to go to his room and sit on his bed, which is covered with beaver pelts from his swamp. He keeps trying to kill all the beavers, but they only come back stronger.

So now he's banging on about his drug dealer—that the guy might be there within an hour—but it's nine thirty and I am wiped out. "Dad, I'm tired, and I don't want to let the dogs out if this guy is going to come up the driveway and run them over."

"Nah, I don't think he's coming. He's very nice. He's gentle. He's a nurse at the local hospital. But . . . he's not the most reliable!" Dad cackles with glee.

Willow comes into the kitchen. I know she smokes pot. Once, I sermonized her at Mom's house: "I would prefer you don't, but I know you do. I am now raising you as a single mother. The neighbors here are peculiar. At any time, they can call Social Services and Child Protection. I can get in trouble. They can make my life difficult. If they took you away from me, I would die. I don't approve of you smoking weed. My dad has smoked for almost fifty years. It is no different than other addictions. But if you are going to smoke pot, don't do it in the house!"

So she smokes pot with her boyfriend, elsewhere. I know Dad is just dying to get high with her. I know because he often asks me, "Will you have a bowl with me?"

And I say, "No, Dad."

And he says, "I guess Tim doesn't want me to invite Willow."

Dad likes to stroke her bare arm and the side of her face and tell her how lovely her skin is. She, in turn, tries to politely move away. He would ask her himself to get high, but . . . I think he is afraid of Tim.

Even though he and Tim smoke the pipe or bong together after dinner—or maybe more often, what do I know—for a long time Tim has told my dad, on our twice-a-year visits, "Don't smoke in front of Willow."

Tim is very reserved in many ways. He's British. The last time we were at Dad's he drank a quart of vodka, smoked a bowl, fell off the stone wall in back, and broke his leg.

As far as I am concerned, if Willow and my dad smoked together, this would probably be the best way to get Willow to quit smoking pot altogether. Dad can be so creepy! He was always on my case to smoke grass with him when I was growing up. Finally I did, when I was eighteen, and I never touched it again.

Dad gets so . . . lascivious. That's right, lascivious. Like, when I was fifteen and I couldn't find a summer job, he tried to get me to enter a wet T-shirt contest. First prize, three hundred dollars. But I would not. At what age are you supposed to get over being scared of your dad entering you in a wet T-shirt contest? He would have had to drive me to that bar, too, since I was too young for a license.

Because Dad is a psychiatrist, he knows how to make you feel you are mentally ill if you don't care for his attentions, or if you don't agree with him, like how he started explaining—as soon as Willow, his granddaughter, turned thirteen—that the legal age for sexual consent should be thirteen, fourteen tops, for girls.

But, whatever. So far Dad and Willow haven't smoked together, and so far Dad hasn't disobeyed Tim's request not to get high in front of her, either. But I guess Tim should have thought harder and told Dad, "And please don't have your drug dealer come over while your granddaughter visits."

I'm tired after the long drive from Ithaca to Albany and then all the way to western Massachusetts. I'm yawning. "Well, Dad, I know you wanted me to meet your dealer. But if he isn't going to stop by, I'm going to sleep."

His house is in the middle of nowhere. Dead center, middle of nowhere. His driveway is, like, half a mile long—a dirt road through the woods, off a dirt road in the woods. We are not talking Montana remote, but it's "a couple hundred acres of private swamp in western Massachusetts" remote.

The nearest shop is a hippie co-op, a three-mile drive away. He built his house, assisted by my brother, almost forty years ago. Everything in it is made by hand: the hanging lamps of stained glass, the massive wooden couch, the hot tub. Even the beaver skin bedspread is from his very own beavers he trapped and drowned.

"Okay! Good night!" Dad says. "I'll see you in the morning. The main thing is, while you're here, you have to call your brother and tell him you are going to inherit the house and he will not be getting anything!"

"Hang on," I say. "You want me to call Sam and tell him you disinherited him?"

"Yes, so you can work out the details of who gets to stay here when I go. He said he wants to live here six months a year and you said that was okay, that you would only stay here half the year."

"But . . . I have to call him and tell him now? You're not dead."

"Oh, it can't just be something he doesn't know about! That wouldn't be right, would it now?"

"Um . . ."

"We will organize this tomorrow. You will call your brother and tell him I have disinherited him and it's all going to you. Of course, I want to remind you: your dogs, they can never come in the house! You will have to design a big fenced area and they will live outside in that area. But you will have to have it specially protected or your dogs will be snatched and eaten. And we can talk about other things. My debts. You are going to have to come up with two hundred twenty thousand dollars to pay the bank, after I die. Do you have that kind of money?"

I head for bed as his eyes narrow. He's trying to get me to stay. "How much money do you have?"

"Oh, gee. Not much!"

"How much?"

I'm gone.

When I get up it's late. "Good morning! You missed my drug dealer visiting last night!" he says to me.

I get a cup of coffee. "What time did he show up?" I ask.

"Oh, I don't know."

Willow comes down. She has the upstairs room, the loft. It didn't used to have a wall on the far side. There was once an open space dropping ten feet to the cement floor of the workroom, and it was right on that edge where the guest bed was placed. Then his last wife, Gigi, wanted the loft room for her loom, so eventually I guess she paid for a wall.

"I just told your mom, she missed the drug dealer coming last night!" he tells her.

"Yeah, Mom," she says accusingly. "You went to sleep too early, Grandpa's dealer had to make some other deliveries but he did get here eventually, right after you went to bed."

"Yes!" Dad says. "He is a nurse, so he had to wait until his shift was over to come by!"

Dad has made pancake mix and we are supposed to cook our own pancakes—he's got a frying pan full of oil a couple of inches deep. I don't want a deep-fried pancake. Tim and Willow don't like pancakes . . . they don't really eat breakfast.

"Nobody wants pancakes?" Dad's pretty angry. He hasn't smoked his morning bowl yet.

I can tell he's trying to keep his grumbling to a minimum, but I am slightly worried. He may lash out at me later, you never know with him. I should have made the pancakes and had everybody sit down and eat them, but honestly . . . I didn't want to get into that trap. If I insist that Willow eat, she will bitch that she doesn't want to. Tim is still asleep. If I wake him, he will get up, eventually, but will not eat anything, either. He will go outside to smoke a ciga-rette. The two of them will be irritated by me. Whatever I do, it's going to be wrong. "I will have a pancake, Dad. Do you want me to cook?"

"You have to call your brother and tell him he will not be in-heriting my property. And I need to know: If you're going to live here, what are you going to do about your dogs?"

"Dad! I haven't even had a cup of coffee yet!" What I do have is a throbbing headache.

"You don't have to sound so vicious, Mom," my daughter says. "Grandpa's just trying to help!" Her tone is of irritation with me and indignant support of old Gramps. That she even gets to con-sider him her grandpa! This guy only came to the city twice in her entire life to see her, his only grandchild. The other times, we had to drive to see him and then stay in a motel.

I remember when I was growing up he used to write me letters, signing them "Julian" and adding in a P.S.: "I don't know whether to call myself your father or your boyfriend." "Dad" was not an op-tion, at least not in his letters.

Tim finally emerges from hibernation. He gets his coffee and smokes a cigarette, which he has to do outside even though Dad smokes marijuana constantly inside. Plus, the house is heated by wood-burning stoves, so nothing about this environment is smoke free, but whatever.

Willow goes out in the canoe. For the moment I have managed to avoid calling my brother, Sam—his only son, the only other child apart from me—to disown him.

dad, guns, and pot

Dad goes up to his room to smoke pot before giving the tour of local colleges. It's Labor Day weekend and there are a lot of colleges in the area for Willow to look at, since she'll be applying soon.

It's already very hot. Willow is cranky in the backseat next to me. "See that house?" Dad says as he drives down the snaky winding road that leads to town. "That house is where my friend Bruce lives. When I got divorced from Gigi, I brought my guns to him. I said, 'Bruce, you keep my guns.'"

"Why did you want him to keep your guns?" I say.

"I didn't feel comfortable having them in the house. I was depressed."

I have heard this story before, when Gigi left him. She was young, maybe five years older than me.

For a long time Dad tried to figure out what had gone wrong with this marriage. He decided that she had left him after twenty-five years because she did not want to look after him when he got old. "Gee, Dad," I said, "do you think maybe you shouldn't have kept saying all the time how great it was that you had a wife who had to go to work and support you while you got to stay home and play?"

"What?" Dad said. "No. No. No. Gigi liked to work."

Nobody else is listening to Dad. I can't help but think: What does that mean, you asked somebody to take your guns because you were "depressed"?

If I had a knife I might say, *Please take my knife from me. I am going to murder someone with it.* I might say, *Please take my knife before I stab myself.* I would not tell people, *Please, take my knife, due to my depression.* I can still have a pair of scissors in my home, even though I am depressed a lot.

"So . . . does your friend still have your guns?"

"Huh? Oh no . . . I got them back. I sawed off my shotgun. But it was crooked, so I asked the chief of police to help me saw it off again. The police chief sawed off the barrel of my shotgun and then . . . the gun didn't work!"

The police chief had sawed off the barrel incorrectly, maybe it was at a slant, I don't know. I don't know what Dad's talking about. He's driving and Willow is cranky, grumbling in the way only a seventeen-year-old can: it's too hot, she doesn't want to go look at colleges, she's got a headache, she's hungry. Tim is in his own zone next to Dad. His body is in there in the front, but . . . he's not exactly there. "And so, I took the shotgun home. Then I went to the gun store and I asked them there, can you fix this gun? Well, the chief of police came in, the same one who had sawed it off incorrectly. And he saw I had the shotgun and he said, 'You can't have that sawed-off shotgun, it's illegal!'"

I'm just not following this.

We do a drive-by of these colleges. There's the University of Massachusetts, Smith College, Amherst College. We get out and walk around, but it's the end of summer and the heat has made the trees shrivel up. There are a few students on campus that Willow doesn't like the look of. She doesn't like the look of any of the campuses.

So it's a lot of driving around from place to place. Tim wants to stop and buy tobacco. We park the car in the center of town.

"So Julian, where can I buy tobacco?" Tim asks.

"At Augie's," I say.

"Augie's!" Dad says. "Augie's closed thirty years ago."

Dad gives Tim directions to some other store. We wait in a fast-food chain place and drink soda. Willow is hungry but she is not going to eat fast food, she wants something different.

And now Dad wants to go back to his house because he is coming down hard. He needs a toke, a puff, a bowl. The hot and hungry and hormonal teen is a bad thing, but I am probably more afraid of the dad. I am trapped, stuck in a pool of rage while everyone around me has a little nuclear meltdown, except Tim, who is oblivious. He's down the block, ambling along. He has no idea that there is multigenerational seething here. The thing is, if he were here and I were the one stalling everyone, he wouldn't notice, either.

He is so lucky! He doesn't have to be in a rage, nor does he appear to notice the rage of others. He gets to live on a nice planet, the one called Planet Oblivion. Is it because he is a Brit? The only time he ever gets angry is when I say something. Then he explains that I am paranoid or wrong.

In all the thirty years I have known him there have only been two people he has announced he didn't like. Two people, out of all the thousands he has met, dined with, talked to. He is friendly, outgoing, warm, interested in others—if only I could be a little bit like him. But no. Try as I might, for me, other human beings are a blend of pit vipers, chimpanzees, and ants, a virtually indistinguishable mass of killer shit-pickers, sniffing their fingers and raping.

At last we are back at Dad's house. Lunchtime!

My family doesn't want berries and yogurt for lunch—we have been coming here for fifteen years as a family and they have never wanted berries and yogurt for lunch, but that's all there has ever been. Somehow Tim and Willow find bread and cheese, fill their plates, and hack away at it.

I am surprised Dad is keeping cool. All my life he went nuts if you didn't sit down and "do" a meal like human beings, with plates and forks and spoons, all at the same time. Dad even dumped one girlfriend, years and years ago, when I was about the age Willow is now, because she went into the kitchen (they were living together by then—Dad made her get rid of her dog first) around lunchtime and she got some food out of the fridge and ate it. Dad didn't say anything at the time. He went off in a black rage. But very shortly after this he threw her out.

Dad is right, though. It is civilized to sit down and eat off plates, together, as a unit. Of course, in all these years I have not been able to get my family to do this at home. I tried, believe me. For years I said to Tim, "Look, we have a little kid, can you get home at six o'clock one night a week so we can have dinner together as a family?" But he never did. The subway was always delayed. Something or other was always happening.

After I visit him, Dad usually sends me a hate letter. I have hundreds of them that go back decades. I already know this one will be about how my family did not sit down for lunch or offer to make lunch, but just went to the refrigerator and got out cheese and ate it with bread!

I'm whimpering now thinking about this future letter. "Dad," I say, "I can't make them sit down for a normal meal, I'm sorry."

Dad nods. I can't believe it, but he seems to accept that it is not my fault. Of course, I will still probably get a hate letter from him.

Sometimes he writes to tell me that my mom was a lousy fuck. Sometimes he writes to tell me I am worthless, that I will never amount to anything. Sometimes he writes to ask me for money to reimburse him for what he spent when I was growing up, or in college.

But for now, I am safe.

Dad goes to his room and great spunky wafts of smoke curl out from under his doorway. When he returns, he is pacified. He is not so high that he's in the giggly touchy-feely state, but he's calmer, happier, not furious with me. I know there will be about an hour's peace this afternoon, then he will have a nap and then it will be time for dinner.

Tim and Willow go out in the canoe. Dad sits out on the deck with me. It is very beautiful to look out over his swamp. "My friend Bruce—the one I gave my guns to when I was depressed—is going to come over for dinner after you go. He's about to have open-heart surgery."

All of Dad's friends are in bad shape. The men come over a few times a week to share a bowl and admire his property. Dad's other friend Josan is dying, but fortunately Josan has a wife with a hundred million dollars who threw him out but rented him an apartment and hired a nurse to look after him.

But Bruce is a young man who's going in for open-heart surgery and is afraid. "He thinks he's going to die on the operating table." Dad laughs maniacally. "But at least I already got my guns back!"

I don't know if he's forgotten that he told me earlier that day, but he launches into the sawed-off shotgun story again.

"I keep it upstairs, in case someone comes out here."

"Who, Dad?"

"If there was a nuclear war, people would come up here from the cities. I have to have a way to protect myself and keep them off.

If someone was looking for drugs. Once, two girls came here. They knocked on the door and said they were looking for their mother."

"They drove miles down the dirt road and then turned onto your dirt driveway and drove another mile until they got to your house? Then they got out of their car and knocked on your door and said they were looking for their mother?"

"Yep."

"Did you know their mother?"

"I don't know."

"Who were they?"

He shrugs.

Before dinner, Dad goes to his room to smoke (the fourth time that day? or maybe the fifth?) and after dinner, when Willow, Tim, and I are sitting there, Dad decides . . . to tell us about his guns.

His sawed-off shotgun is illegal, he keeps it under his bed—I think—and maybe some other guns up in his closet? He is just . . . on and on, and I am learning he has a lot of guns, how many I don't know. But I do know that he gave his guns away and got them back because it is the fourth time that day I am hearing this story.

The evening passes. I don't know what we do, do we play Scrabble? Are we all sitting on Dad's bed on the beaver blanket, watching a movie on his giant TV screen? Dad starts talking about his guns again. He's mumbling, to himself, and it dawns on me: Daddy's nuts!

I am in the middle of the woods with my kid, who is applying to college, with this crazed old man who has drug dealers stopping by and can't stop smoking pot and talking about his guns. He's nuts and dangerous! It takes me a long time to put all this together. I am very slow to understand people. But I know I've got to get my family out of here.

"Just then," Dad says, "the chief of police came in and said,

'You can't sell that sawed-off shotgun! It doesn't work. It's illegal to sell a gun that doesn't work.'"

What law is that? I thought you couldn't sell a sawed-off shotgun because having a sawed-off shotgun is illegal, whether it works or not.

There is something really wrong. I have brought my family here, and even though my father hasn't shot anybody before (as far as I know), that doesn't mean he might not feel the urge to shoot someone now. Or this "unreliable" drug dealer might come back and Dad might decide to shoot him, or the drug dealer might decide to shoot back and my family is caught in the crossfire. Or even worse, Dad might think he hears an intruder and shoot my kid. Later, after the shooting, he might tell the police, "I thought someone broke in, I forgot completely I had houseguests!" What are they going to do, put an eighty-three-year-old in jail?

This is actually a highly possible situation. You don't know my father.

I go downstairs. "Tim, we have got to get out of here. The guns, the guns, the guns, the drug dealer. You want to have your drug dealer come over while you have houseguests, including your granddaughter? Just say, 'I left something at a friend's house and he's stopping by to drop it off.' You don't keep saying, 'My drug dealer is coming! My drug dealer is coming!' And what if this dealer—a nurse at the hospital!—was in trouble with the police and turned in his clients and they came out here and took Willow?"

For once, Tim kind of agrees.

"I'm not kidding. I am afraid. We have to get out of here," I say.

I would not put anything past Dad. No matter how much he asks, I can't find him a gallery! I am barely surviving; it's hard enough getting my books published. If you want a gallery you have to go and schmooze the right people. It was bad enough that my grandmother was always asking me to get her a show for her paint-ings. There are two parts to art: the work and the business side. You have to do both, right? Sigh. It doesn't matter. All I know is, at this point, what's Dad got to lose? His artworks—the sculptures, one of which, he will explain to you, represents two figures with their heads connected, having an orgasm, the free-form stained-glass lamps the size of dinosaurs, hanging from the ceiling—have never gotten any attention, and he's now in his eighties, so what's he got to lose?

But where are we going to go? It's the middle of the night . . . well, 11 P.M., but there are no motels for miles—let alone one that will accept eight poodles. (I'm not saying I'm normal, either.)

"Okay, so what do you want to do?" Tim says. "I don't think your father is going to shoot us, but . . . I don't want to stay here, either."

"We'll have to stay here overnight, but I'm afraid. Could you please go talk to my dad?"

Tim returns after some time. "Your father wants to see you. He wants to know what's going on."

"No! I don't want to discuss this. Tell him he has to give you the gun he keeps under the bed and put it in the trunk of the car. Then I can sleep at least."

Tim comes down with a couple of .22s and another gun. We go to the car together while he puts them in the trunk. "Where's the sawed-off shotgun, Tim?"

"Your dad says he doesn't have a sawed-off shotgun under the bed."

Dad comes out. "What's going on?"

"Dad, I need you to give me your sawed-off shotgun from under the bed."

"I don't have one under the bed."

"Then where do you have it?"

"On top of the closet."

"Give me the sawed-off shotgun, Dad!"

So I get some of the guns stashed away for the night. Probably not all.

In the morning we give the guns back and get ready to leave. That's when Dad's girlfriend arrives, as we're trying to rush off. "Oh, what a shame not to see you. Is there nothing we can do or say to get you to stay?" she says.

"My daughter's hysterical!" Dad says.

"No, I'm not hysterical," I tell him.

"She is hysterical," he tells the others. "I have always had guns. You knew. I had to get a gun, back when I was still in practice and a former patient began making threats. It was to protect myself."

I could have reminded him, "Dad, she came to you for her sexual problems and you fucked her. And she was making suicidal threats, not threats against you."

But he probably would have denied it, because smoking pot makes you forget things, and also because he's fucked so many of his female patients, he wouldn't have remembered which one it was.

"You would never be able to live out here," he says. "Not two miles from here, a seventy-year-old man was shot and killed. You can't live here, not without a gun."

SO, NATURALLY, DAD DISOWNS ME. He decides to give his estate to the Audubon Society instead.

my mom

My mother is lying on her side with her diapers full of shit. She was a professor of English at Cornell University and an award-winning poet when she retired less than three years ago.

It is not possible she is going to read this—or, if she does, she is going to read the same line over and over again, like she did the other day from *The New Yorker*. "'Manuel Uno is two years old and already five feet high at the withers.'" She read it aloud. Then she laughed and said, "Who is Manuel Uno?" and read it over again. It was something about an aurochs, and she asked me, "What's an aurochs?" I explained that, according to the article she was reading to me, it was some type of primitive or prehistoric cow.

Then she read it out loud, again, laughed, and said, "What's an aurochs?"

After she took her first serious fall, I left my life in the city and came to her house in upstate New York to look after her. There was feces everywhere. It was on the floor and the walls and the refrigerator. I took her to a doctor. "My mom has had chronic diarrhea for many months," I said.

"Have you given her Pepto-Bismol?" the doctor asked. "You can try it in tablet or liquid, available at your local drugstore."

She kept falling. I got home health care. Things got worse. No doctors helped.

The home health aide quit. She put a big sign on the front door that stated: "I did not want to tell your mother, but I had to quit because there was FECES EVERYWHERE."

My mom had gone out and read the sign. She was hysterical. "Why did she have to put that up?" she cried. The whole neighborhood saw it.

I put her in a nursing home.

My sister-in-law Veronica told everyone, "Tama thought it was 'necessary' to put Phyllis in a nursing home." She's married to my brother, Sam. They live in Alabama. She sits at home and watches talk shows and soap operas. He is a doctor. After work he does the shopping, cooking, and cleaning.

I didn't *think* it was necessary to put my mom in a home. It *was* necessary.

Now I go to her nursing home every day. There is a woman there who staggers around, holds back tears, and repeatedly asks, "Where is my daughter? Do you know where my daughter is?" No matter how many times you tell her, "Your daughter is at work, she will be here this evening," she still asks. There is another woman who used to be a concert pianist. She wears a big bib, with pictures of kittens or puppies, tucked right up under her chin. She wanders around shouting, "When is dinner? I'm hungry!" They could have just finished eating, or it could be two in the afternoon, but still she is in a rage about having nothing to eat. At any time someone is going around with a tea trolley containing tiny gray muffins or canned diced peaches with whipped topping or Jell-O. They stuff her and stuff her, but the woman still yells for food.

At lunch the residents get milk that's pink. I hope it's strawberry flavored. Lunch is the big meal there. They have a cup of soup
and then the main dish, chicken with mashed potatoes and a green
vegetable—well, greenish. There are group meetings for the more
functional residents where they're asked what they'd like to see on
the menu. Of the ones who can articulate, some want roast beef
and some want pizza.

Mary, one of the residents, spends mealtime diddling the
sugar. She takes off the top of the container and might dump it on
her food or in her glass of water, then stirs and stirs until the water
is cloudy and adds some cream or mashed potatoes and takes a sip.

This is an upscale place, too. I don't mean it is super fancy, but
it is expensive. It doesn't stink the way some old people's homes
do, except in my mother's room, where it usually smells like shit
because her diapers are full and she just goes in them all the time.

I am trapped.

a supermarket
in ithaca

I hated being in Mom's house when Mom was still living there. I hated living in upstate New York. I had to get out. My only escape was . . . the supermarket. That is what I did for fun. Not going out—to restaurants, bars, nightclubs, openings, premieres— because as far as I knew, there was nowhere worth going! I didn't have friends there and Mom panicked if I was away for more than a half hour, frantic, ready to call the police.

I would make up an excuse for something we needed, just to get away. But then I had to get in the car. I had to drive that 1995 Mazda, and every single time it smashed itself into the side of the garage. I have a driver's license but had lived in the city my whole life and never drove. There are subways in New York City that take you from point A to point B, more or less. There are taxis. There are buses. There's nowhere to park a car. Not driving is normal if you live in New York City.

When I first got upstate I just sat in the car in the garage shaking. I couldn't even start it. What if I did and it decided to go into the wall? (It did.) What if it decided to back up over a person? So far, no, but who knew what it was going to do?

When Mom drove, she always explained that it took two people to drive, and my job was to look right when we came to a stop sign, while she looked left. Then we discussed whether there was any oncoming traffic. The discussion took a long time. Then she had to check on my side, to make sure. I had a license but had always known I would never be able to drive. Now I was forced to.

The supermarket wasn't exactly a fun destination. It was just a place to go. Actually, that supermarket got me so agitated that I was ready to kill. There were signs like this one:

You don't have to put "cold cereal" and "hot cereal" on two separate lines! Just put "cereal"! Why do you have pancake syrup in this aisle? Why? It belongs in the baking goods aisle! And what is "diet"?

Presumably, the manager was severely mentally ill. I assumed he was male, because you didn't see many women working there except the registers or those little free-sample stands trying to get you to buy frozen strawberry Slurpees with agave sweetener made right there in a blender and served on a pita chip. Why couldn't I just feel sorry for the manager?

Because he listed "canned soup" and "soup cups" as different categories, that's why. Because his store had one aisle with "water," another with "beverages," and a third for "soda" (with "root beer" getting its own listing). Plus "juice" in one aisle, "boxed juice" in another.

Also, although there were dozens of brands of salsa in that supermarket, there was no hot salsa, only mild and medium. The manager must not have liked hot salsa—the only decent kind, in my opinion—and therefore assumed no one else liked it, either.

Aisle 12 had beer. But aisle 3 had "cold beer" and "imported beer." Did a lot of customers come in and say, "Where can I find the cold beer that is not American?"

And to round out the beverages in aisle 3: INSECTICIDE. Not a winning combination. I couldn't believe there weren't other people staggering around mumbling and cursing like I was. Didn't anyone else want to demand to see this manager? Had no one registered a query or a complaint: Why was "Hispanic" in one aisle but "Mexican" in another?

I went to the supermarket to get the hell out of my mom's house and found myself pushing a cart around, ready to go postal.

My real mission was going to the "bulk candy" aisle to get my mom the sour balls she liked. There was a man who lived in that aisle. He opened each bin, licked his fingers, touched the candy, fondled it . . . and left. Asperger's? OCD? Plain weird? I don't know, but my mom was addicted to these colored hard candies, so I had to get them. For years she had gone to the supermarket just about every day to fill a bag; she wouldn't eat the red ones or the orange ones—only the white, yellow, and green, green being her favorite. But there were hardly ever any green.

When I was still living in Brooklyn I used to have the hard candy shipped to her—five, ten pounds at a time—in between my visits every few weeks. Sometimes my mom would call me in a panic. "Where are my sour balls? I can't find them!"

"But Mom, I shipped you ten pounds a little while ago."

I just thought: Wow, Mom eats a lot of sour balls. Or that one day I would open a closet and a vast supply would fall out. Finally my brother called me and said, "Don't give her that candy! It's bad for her teeth."

That's when I figured out that her panic directly coincided with his twice-a-year visits. He was not only tossing the candy, but not telling her, and thereby inflicting an extra dose of dementia.

He had done the same to his own his father-in-law, who was ninety and liked ice cream. The father-in-law also had a live-in home aide, so he was well looked after, but my brother and sister-in-law went to court and got guardianship, saying the aide was a drug addict and prostitute, and placed him in a rental property. They bought ice cream and they put it in the freezer. And then they put a chain and padlock on it. I remember saying to Dad, "What bothers me is that they put a chain around the freezer to stop him from eating ice cream. I mean, you can't eat all the ice cream you want when you're a kid because you're not allowed, and then you can't eat all the ice cream you want when you're an adult because you worry about getting fat. Surely by the time a person gets to be ninety-three, they should be allowed to eat as much ice cream as they want. If he was going to die at, say, ninety-six, who would say, 'Yeah, but he might have lived to be ninety-eight if only he hadn't eaten so much ice cream'?"

Anyway, every time I went to the supermarket, Mom had fallen by the time I came back to the house, stuck on the ground, unable to get up. Sometimes she demanded hard candy while she was lying down. "Mom! Let me help you up!"

"First bring me a lime sour ball."

life in ithaca

Before my mom went into the nursing home, I would go up to Ithaca from Brooklyn a few times a month and scrape the wrappers and the old gum and the remains of anything else off the bedroom floor. There was always a layer a few inches deep. I would work and work on clearing out a space. I would put a wastebasket next to her bed. "Ma! When you unwrap a candy, can't you put the wrapper in the bin and not the floor?"

But she never did.

When I left her house the floor was clean, but by the time I came back a few weeks later the floor was covered. There was just so much stuff.

Some people maybe have a drawer where there is tape neatly organized in a box, and a drawer below that with batteries organized by size. These people do not have a drawer containing fifty eye pencil stubs, a wind-up metal chicken, a thousand free address labels with pictures of kittens from some Humane Society, and a small lead sap with a leather handle to hit someone over the head with if they break into your house in the middle of the night. The sap had belonged to my grandfather, who was a parole officer in New York City, like, seventy years ago. My mom kept it, though, because where were you ever going to find one these days? It wasn't like there was a single store where you could just go in and say, "I would like to buy a sap." That meant, in my mother's opinion, it was a valuable collectible. This was the kind of drawer my mom had.

When I moved in I wanted to get the place cleaned up, but there was so much stuff. I couldn't get through to the bed in the room I was staying in. I had to tunnel my way. It took me three years to finally get the place cleared out.

The back door was crumbling and air was rushing in under it. For years I had been telling her to get it fixed, but she always said, "You can't find anybody around here to do any work." I figured what she really meant was that there were people around who would do jobs, but she didn't want them in her house (even if they could get in, with the gum wrappers and half-eaten sour balls).

Winter was coming and I was panicking about the door. In Brooklyn, you have central heating. You have a super. The super may not be competent, he may not be any good at fixing things, but you have that incompetent man, who must obey your commands, as your very own—more obedient than a husband because you tip him at Christmas.

I went on local listings on the computer, and at random called a number for a handyman: Melvyn answered.

Melvyn drove a rusted pickup. He was short and weighed about 250 pounds, most of it in his center. He had on overalls. He had a beard and a red face. He breathed heavily, so heavily and slowly that he seemed to be saying with every exhalation, *I don't want to fix your door,* and with every inhalation, *I'm not going to fix your door,* like some kind of Buddhist chant or yoga breathing exercise.

But he said he would do the job.

"When do you think you can start?"

"Start?" He stood staring at the back door, wheezing. "Oh. I don't know about that." It was Monday. "How about Thursday? I could get here on Thursday. Or Friday. Or I could come next week."

"How about Thursday?"

"What?" Melvyn said. "Um. I'm going to have to check with my wife. She works nights as a nurse. I've been out of work. So I thought I would put up an ad. I didn't think anybody would respond, especially not so soon. I'm going to check with my wife and I'll let you know."

You could tell he was somewhat disappointed I wanted him to do the job. And I did not think I would see Melvyn again.

On Thursday Melvyn returned. He started to work, first by looking at the back door. I left him hard at it and went upstairs. After about a half hour, Melvyn yelled, "Um, ma'am?"

I went downstairs.

"Ma'am?"

"Yes, Melvyn. What's up?"

"I don't feel good." He whimpered and had a pained expression.

"What's the matter?"

"Did you know . . . you got a dead squirrel out there in the back?"

"A dead squirrel?"

"I had to go out back to get some air. You got a dead squirrel and it made me sick. I think maybe your dogs ate it. Something ate it. When I saw it, I threw up. You know them kids were over to the house the other day, they ate a lot of candy and they been sick. Maybe I got something from them. I'm going home."

He had removed the back door. Now there was a big hole where the door had been. He began gathering up all his tools.

I followed him to the front door. "Melvyn . . . I . . . Do you think you could clean up your vomit? It's a very small yard and I don't want the dogs finding it."

He seemed surprised. "What? Oh . . . No. It's okay. I cleaned it up already."

He got in his truck and drove off.

I went to see. What had made Melvyn ill? Off in a corner was a small, decaying squirrel corpse. It was true I had not seen it before. It was very old and there was almost nothing left to it. It had dried completely and was bald except for a small strip of fur on the tail. It looked like a young squirrel that had died maybe a few years before. It was not a fresh roadkill or covered with flies or maggots.

The dogs gathered around me, but the little cadaver was so old it was of no interest to them. I grabbed a plastic bag, wrapped the squirrel in it, and threw it in the garbage. I checked briefly but I did not see any vomit.

You wouldn't say Melvyn was charming or quirky. He was just a big, fat, vomiting, gray-bearded guy. He was not an Ithaca guy.

Ithaca is an academic, university town. It has a cooperative health food store and vegetarian and vegan options. It has jazz concerts and fiber arts festivals. Ithaca is in Tompkins County. Melvyn came from another county.

a bit about
schuyler county

Melvyn came from Schuyler County, where all the men drive trucks and have facial hair, tattoos, and hunt deer. Schuyler County does not have a health food store. Schuyler County has a Cheez Doodle supply center—Walmart. Schuyler County is where, if you have an old bathtub you do not want, you throw it in the woods.

I did not know then that in less than two years I would move to Schuyler County and buy a run-down Greek Revival farmhouse that had graffiti on the wall that said KILL MOM, and I did not know that I would get a boyfriend like Melvyn, only a lot cuter, and I would drive around in this tattooed construction worker's truck while he showed me spots where he hunted deer up in the woods.

But I did know—even then, in Ithaca—that living in upstate New York wasn't any year in Provence with charming quirky local characters eating great French cuisine. It was barfing fat guys and bizarre supermarket managers who put insecticide in the beverage aisle.

Okay, could I have organized a supermarket? Probably not. I would never even have gotten a job in a supermarket. I'm just saying.

In Ithaca, there are vegetarian academics who teach morons at the prestigious university.

In Schuyler County, there are locals with guns and tractors who are mostly unemployed. The women work; they have menial positions in supermarkets and in nursing homes at minimum wage and they have unemployed husbands. A lot of the unemployed husbands have lawn tractors. You can tell they are unemployed because on any day of the week they are out there mowing a dead lawn, around and around. Sometimes I drive up the same road for a week and the same guy is out there every day.

They had some of the shortest lawns on the planet in upstate New York.

Forget Provence, this wasn't even the mountains of West Virginia, where they had local traditions like bluegrass music with men playing the fiddle and moonshine and a charming accent. Here it was Top 20 country-western radio only: in the barns, in the trucks, and at home. Country-WESTern. This was *not* the West.

Schuyler County imported everything. There was no local indigenous music. There were no shaved truffles or hearty cassoulets. The local diet is on view in the shopping carts: twenty-pound bags of sour-cream-and-onion potato chips, sodas (and also "root beer"), hot dogs, and maybe some ice cream or boxed cake, all of which might be as old as the bird's nests used in that Chinese soup, what is it, thousand-year-old soup or something? "Preservative" is the county's number-one food ingredient.

In Schuyler County, when a cupcake shop opened—a concept already at least ten years old in New York City—they baked the cupcakes using Betty Crocker cake mix. It was considered upscale.

Little did I know this would soon be the cuisine I was going to have to learn to cook. I like a challenge, though.

Schuyler County Salad
1 lb. cooked macaroni
1 2-lb. jar Miracle Whip Dressing
1 shaker of salt

The only things the men in the area actually enjoy, if they are true locals, are snowmobiling and hunting. The regional costume for men is trucker's caps and greasy Carhartts and baggy Dickies, out of which protrude their proud guts. With everybody poor or unemployed the stores are always empty until—come fall—the hunting departments of the sporting goods stores are packed. The men turn into shoppers for guns, the latest in camouflage fashion, foot warmers, portable deer blinds, and expensive soaps to wash their clothes in, so they didn't have any scent to scare off the deer.

At Mom's first nursing home there was a male nurse who told me, "I hunt for sustenance. To feed the family." That's what they all say—they are doing it for "sustenance." No, they are not. By the time these men buy the guns and the ammo and the night vision goggles and the camouflage to hide themselves and the Day-Glo vests so the other hunters don't shoot them, and buy gas for their pickups that get, I don't know, ten, fifteen miles to the gallon, shoot a deer, lug it to the butcher, have it butchered—forget it! You are looking at meat that probably cost ten, twelve bucks a pound—and for what? Not only does nobody need to eat meat all the time, but venison jerky, venison burger, venison steak—that stuff doesn't taste good! I don't care if you add chili and cumin or if you put it in a slow cooker with red wine and onions, it is gamy and stringy and has a metallic taste of fear you can't ever quite cover up.

an inhabitant of schuyler county

I used to go to sleep every night and pray that when I woke I would have become vegan, or at least vegetarian. But life doesn't necessarily turn out the way you want, and I would find myself at the stove, cooking bacon again.

I can say that it is morally better to be a vegetarian since you are not making anything else suffer in order to keep your own suffering going. There are people like the Jains, in India, who eat nothing but leaves and leaf by-products and have to make sure there are no bugs on them. They avoid harming animals, even to the point of getting up to gently brush the streets before dawn so no one steps on an insect. There are Orthodox Jews so religious that all of Crown Heights was thrown into a tizzy when they realized the water contained organisms that were some kind of microscopic crustacean—not kosher.

These philosophies may be too extreme, but what do I know? Since I eat meat, I cannot tell others what to do. I do know that a cow—or a sheep—is not going to survive by itself out in the wild. The types of cows we have now are not aurochs. They need silage, shelter, worm paste. They are feeble-minded, survival-wise, or we would see cows proud and free in the forest.

Same with sheep. You can't just take some sheep and say, I release you! You are free now! Run wild! The sheep is not going to survive out there. After it rains, it is just going to topple over from the weight of its own wet, unshorn fur. It's going to get caught in barbed wire and bleat to death.

The one thing—of course!—no one up here could tolerate was any suggestion that guns shouldn't be legal. They would just about blow your head off at the very mention of the topic.

At first, when I arrived in Schuyler County, I thought I should get to know a little bit about the place. I found an ad in the paper:

What an interesting event to attend! I thought. Local culture. So I went.

The Interlaken Sports Club was in a metal building, miles away from my house, in the middle of a field. People lined up to buy their tickets, and it was sold out by four thirty. Everyone waited at long tables until the command to get our food was given. Set up on long steam tables were approximately fifty special dishes, served buffet style in aluminum trays, made from items with no stated provenance or history. Where did the stuff come from? Ancient food from ancient freezers? Roadkill? All dishes were created by the members of the Interlaken Sports Club.

There was squirrel and rabbit stew; there was opossum gumbo, turtle soup, frog legs, moose stew; and then there was venison: venison sausage, venison lasagna, venison pot roast, venison hamburgers, and deep-fried venison balls.

I went to this event all by myself, way the hell out in the middle of nowhere, in the middle of winter, too.

Did it make me change my mind about venison?

A lot of things changed.

As soon as I moved up there I became involved with a construction worker. A little bit about my boyfriend:

When he leaves, there are always little piles of his bullet casings on the windowsill, or on my underwear on the floor, and his rifles lean against the walls in every corner.

He has a cabin full of heads of what he shot. He has a mustache and wears those worker boots and those Carhartts and if he's not carrying a rifle, it's a chain saw.

Okay, he is very cute. He's all muscles and tattoos and wears T-shirts that advertise motor oil or say things like DEAD DEER WALKING. He's got a big truck, it's a black and chrome GMC Sierra 4x4 and he puts on Aerosmith or "She Thinks My Tractor's Sexy." He cranks up the volume and he drives me to Walmart and while I shop he waits in his truck—just like real locals, where the men wait in the truck while the wives or girlfriends go in!

The local men never go in, either because it is a sissy thing to do or because they are like rare, elusive birds who cannot leave their indigenous habitat, too shy, never seen outside their natural environs—whatever. They don't leave their trucks. Or their barns, or tractors, or recliners.

He wakes up at 6 A.M. (5 in hunting season), smokes a Kool in bed, and then jumps up. He has to chop down trees or grind stumps or he's off to snowplow the shopping plaza parking lots for twenty hours. Unless it's hunting season. Then he walks miles through the snow to sit in a tree until a male deer with at least ten points runs by after a doe in heat. And he shoots it.

He used to race stock cars, he had two kids with two different girls by the time he was seventeen years old, he's got a dick down to his knees.

It's disgusting. I mean, I am an old person; I am fifty-seven! You should just not have a boyfriend when you get to be that old, right? You should not be having sex.

But when he grabs me by the arm and pulls me across the room and before I know it my pants are down around my ankles and he's got me bent over a chair, what am I going to do, complain about it?

On the other hand, he can be so, so, so mean. Not, like, he hits me, but he has issues.

He would not go with me to the Wild Game Dinner at the Interlaken Sports Club, for example. And he will not eat a "farm-fresh egg" from the local produce place where the woman has very old chickens; she never kills them. These are happy chickens and lay eggs rarely because they are old. You have to order a dozen in advance, and their yolks are bright orange. He only wants pale ones from the supermarket, collected from the Factory of Suffering Chickens.

He would not leave a job site, even though it was 7 P.M. on one of the only warm days in six months, to go on a walk with me through the forest. He said he had broken up with his girlfriend, but then he claimed he had to go with her to a Christmas expo and convention in a nearby city for five days in order to drive back all the angels and Christmas tree accessories she was stocking for her Christmas shop.

Okay, mostly I can't stand my husband, but (right now at least) *I hate* my boyfriend!

My life has turned into a sweater with a hole in it: whether it's raveling or unraveling, it doesn't make any difference.

time in brooklyn

I'm not saying life was any better back in Brooklyn. I couldn't stand it there, either. Like when the incident of the doorman molestation occurred—I don't know—ten or twenty years ago?

Achmed, the doorman in my apartment building, was young, always friendly and nice, sometimes maybe too nice. He kissed me on the cheek at Christmas, and it wasn't just a peck on the cheek—he kind of grabbed me and rubbed up against me. There were other things that should have been clues.

On Mother's Day, Achmed gave me a huge bunch of flowers. I mean, this bouquet was beautiful, it wasn't some tired bunch of flowers from a Korean deli. It was a lot nicer than any bouquets my husband ever gave me. Don't get me wrong, I like flowers from a corner bodega, too. But this was from a fancy florist, white lilies and tuberoses, in a vase with tissue paper. They were in a box at the front desk. Achmed was looking at me, doggy-style. At first I was like, Holy crap, who sent me these beautiful flowers!

"I did!" he said.

I just didn't know what to do—laugh, cry? It was so great to get this gorgeous bouquet of flowers, but . . . they weren't from my husband, they weren't from a possible admirer, they were from the Egyptian doorman who was young enough to be my son.

It reminded me of how, one time, my friend Paige got a fancy invitation from her cleaning woman, inviting her to tea at the Duke and Duchess of somebody or other. So she asked Andy Warhol to join her. They went to tea at this Duke and Duchess's place in New York City and then Andy said, "Gee, Paige, this is great! Who invited us to this tea?"

"Why, my cleaning woman Helen invited us," Paige said. Then she introduced Andy to Helen, her housekeeper.

Andy was really mad. He wanted to have tea with the Duke and Duchess of whatever it was, but it spoiled it for him when it turned out he had been invited by Paige's cleaning woman.

Achmed had a thirteen-year-old daughter who was a country-western singer. He would tell me about this daughter and the talent shows she was entering at the time. Once there was a building Christmas party and his daughter performed, a huge girl playing the mandolin with a tiny partner on slide guitar, playing "Achy Breaky Heart." Many building residents and workers did a line dance where the lobby had been cleared between the Christmas tree and the food and the menorah.

A lot of the residents were old lefties and academics, who had bought their apartments when the building went co-op in the early eighties. They didn't line-dance, but they did dance to "The Tennessee Waltz." It was very impressive, especially for me. In college I had failed ballroom dancing. I actually got an F for not being able to waltz.

Anyway, one night Achmed the doorman called on the intercom and said he was on his break and asked if I wanted to hang out with him in the boiler room. The boiler room was behind a marked door that said no one was allowed in unless you worked in the building, so I was kind of excited to see what was behind it.

"Okay, sure," I said.

I caught a glimpse of myself on the way out. I was pretty shabby. "How old do I look?" I said to Willow.

"Well, you look like you might be younger than sixty," she said.

I went to the basement. Inside this boiler room were gigantic, huge, riveted—gosh, I don't know—boilers? And this area was two stories high at least, and very hot and noisy, and it was like being in a submarine engine room. From around the corner I heard Achmed tell me to come in.

I entered the porters' and doormen's lounge. There was a giant TV, a smaller TV, a big sofa, a refrigerator, rugs, chairs—it was messy and yet a place to hang out. I guess like the basement of some sixties home or something for the kids. Or maybe like some of the nightclubs I used to go to back in the early eighties.

Achmed wanted me to have some cognac, Ukrainian cognac.

I said no because I had my glass of wine with me. Then he turned off the sound on the TV, which was playing a movie with giant cartoon rats.

He sat next to me on the couch donated by some building tenant who had remodeled and who had also given him the cognac. "Are you sure you don't want the cognac?" he kept asking me. I did not know at that time that Ukraine is known for its fine cognac. I said, "No." This time he got out the cognac and poured himself a large glass.

Then I tried to ask him questions—what his wife did, about his father staying with him. His father, he said, had been visiting but was about to go back to Egypt. His wife came from Peru and they had met online. He had worked in the building for eight years or something and was a member of the doormen's union.

Even though I kept asking him questions, he leaned on me and started to kiss me. I protested, saying we were friends, and tried to leave, but he followed me to the door, once again grabbed me, and tried to kiss me on the mouth.

It was not really possible to pry him off with ease, but eventually I did.

When I went upstairs Willow said I had been gone ten minutes. To me it seemed like several days in the boiler room.

I suppose I was foolish to go there, but I had truly thought we were friends and that he was fond of me. I was almost fifty-five years old and had I removed my clothing, I can assure you he would have screamed. I'd had an operation where they removed a tumor the size of a five-month fetus, which left me misshapen. Then afterward, stupidly, I went to an old boyfriend's wife who was a plastic surgeon to get liposuction and try to even out the lumps. Do not go to an ex-boyfriend's wife for lipo! Not when that ex-boyfriend has never gotten over you. I swear, she *added* fat deposits on me when I was under anesthesia.

In any event, I was not inclined to do anything with Achmed. But then the next day he followed me into the elevator.

Certainly there was a period when I would very much have liked to have an affair. But not then. I was wearing a skirt, and Achmed scuttled up behind me into the elevator. Just as the doors were about to close, he stuck his hand around the edge of my underpants and right up in there.

I was enraged. I mean, this was no white-glove building, but they could have at least insisted on latex. How could I have misread the whole thing so drastically? Now, for the rest of my life, I was going to have to go past a doorman who might either follow me into the elevator and try to stick his hand down my pants, or, even if he didn't, look at me and think, There goes the one from 16A I felt up.

I didn't want to get the guy fired. He had a wife and the singer and another daughter. His father didn't speak any English. Life was hard.

Plus, I couldn't think of him trying to supply me with Ukrainian cognac without remembering that it was in Kiev where I'd lost my mother in a crowd, eight years earlier. I was with her and Willow in a Folkloric Tourist Market, and when I turned around Mom was gone. She had no money, no credit card, no passport, no copy of the address of where we were staying. Willow and I spent the entire day looking for her, and it wasn't until night had fallen and it was raining that I gave up. I think Mom was losing it even back then.

I did find her eventually, five or six hours later, thanks to the U.S. Embassy. She was having drinks with the vice-consul at an American jazz bar.

family relations

The roots falling out of my family had commenced years before my not talking to my brother Sam and Dad disinheriting him. First, Sam got into an argument with Dad when Dad visited him and tried to smoke marijuana. Sam asked him to please smoke it outside since he had terrible allergies and the smoke bothered him, and this pissed off my father.

In my mother's case, the rift with Sam's wife began when my mom called to thank Sam and Veronica for a Mother's Day present they had sent. According to my mother, Veronica picked up the phone and said angrily, "You should thank your son, don't thank me!" Then she launched into a shrill diatribe of complaints against Mom. It was out of context and vicious, too. I was not privy to hearing this because I was not there at the time. I myself had long ceased calling my brother, knowing that his wife was right there, listening to every word on speakerphone—or extension—but never saying anything.

I had my own issues with Veronica, and not only because she really hurt my mom's feelings. My mom said Veronica told her she was a hunchback. My mom cried. This is nothing against hunchbacks but my mom was not a hunchback. She had a little osteoporosis. Even if my mom *was* a hunchback, do you go around saying, "Hahaha! You are a *hunchback*!"

For me, though, the trouble started many years ago when Tim and I went to visit them outside Boston. When it was time to go I went to the closet to get our coats, but they were gone. And I said, "Hey, where are our coats?"

"I put them out in the garage," said Veronica, "because they smelled. Sam is allergic."

I did not have an odoriferous coat. And I did not want to visit people who said I did.

Of course Veronica was even worse the last time my mother went to see them. Sam and Veronica accused my mother of wearing perfume. And when my mother said, "I am not! I knew you were sensitive to odor and so I deliberately did not wear any perfume," they did not believe her. They ransacked her items and went through everything she had brought with her to find her perfume, which they assumed she had hidden after she applied it. But she hadn't.

I DON'T KNOW WHY TOLSTOY said "All happy families are alike." First of all, he couldn't have spent much time with any family or he would have found out that there is no such thing as a happy family. I have met happy families, and after a few minutes one of them takes you off to one side to explain the real truth.

Tolstoy was busy writing or touring the countryside visiting serfs, which caused his wife unhappiness since she had to spend all her time fixing up her husband's novels and raising eight children, even though her husband the count was giving away all their money to the serfs he hung out with, faster than he could impregnate her.

I am pretty sure you can't find one family on the entire planet where there is not one family member at war with another.

In Schuyler County I made a lot of new friends through Newell Farm, where I rode. Everyone seemed to have a normal family, until they started confiding. There was "Dressage" Amy: her sister came down with a virus that overnight left her paralyzed and barely able to speak. So her youngest son took her to Canada and lived with her in an apartment. They had the woman's Social Security disability money to live on, but this son said, "I have to take care of my mom all the time, and that's not fair!" Because he wanted more money from other family members.

But they did not want to give him their own money because the last time they did that he tied his mother to the toilet and took the extra money and went to Toronto and hired a prostitute. I believe he also bought some drugs, but I do not know the full details, only that he forgot he had tied his mother to the toilet and sometime between twenty-four and forty-eight hours went by before he got back and untied her, unsoiled but greatly dehydrated.

Or my friend "Trail Rider" Melanie. When she was young her mother died. Her younger sister disappeared for years to live in a trailer, where she had many children by different men. Then Melanie's aunt called to tell her her father had died. They hadn't been that close, but it still came as a shock. One day, about ten years after the death of her father, she thought she would call her father's wife, who had inherited all the money, to find out if she knew where her sister was. And her father answered the phone. He was not dead! He just didn't care enough about her to bother calling.

Meanwhile, of course, Melanie was in recovery from breast cancer and her husband and her mother-in-law (with whom they lived) would not let her drive a car or ride a bike, because she had suffered concussions in the past, and so they did not let her have those privileges. The area that they lived in was not near any stores and it snowed most of the time, and when it wasn't snowing it flooded. She was quite trapped there, with her mother-in-law, whom she was not permitted to address by her first name. And her husband and her mother-in-law made her dog wear underpants in the house because it was a short-haired dog with an up-curling tail and they did not like to look at its anus.

So each family has its troubles and woes, and in some way all unhappy families are alike, because as far as I can tell there really aren't any happy ones, at least not fully or all the time.

In my father's case, it was dislike of my brother's wife that caused him to disinherit my brother, and then he turned his back on me when I left his house after realizing just how many weapons he had lying around—well, that and my objection to the drug dealer.

By the way, the morning I fled his home, I returned his munitions and wrote him a note:

Dear Dad,
    You tell me:
    1. Your drug dealer is "gentle" but "unreliable"
    2. You brought up and discussed your sawed-off shotgun FIVE
        TIMES at great length during the course of one day.

There was no way to explain anything to him. Years before, he'd gotten an acre or two of land as some kind of settlement for a lawsuit (he and his past wife were always embroiled in lawsuits of one sort or another), so he sold the land for something like five grand. Then, when he complained that my brother could have bought land and lived near him instead of moving to Alabama, I said, "Right, Dad, but if you had wanted your son to stay near you—your son who helped you build your house!—you might have rewarded him with the acre of land you got in a settlement, instead of selling it for five grand!"

"It was two acres of land and it sold for five thousand per acre!" Dad said.

I'm telling you, you just couldn't argue with him.

When I went back recently, I think Dad was happy things were going so badly for me, and that I had ended up totally broke and living up in the middle of some bizarre black hole of the United States without culture, and I think when my brother called, he encouraged him against me.

My brother is highly litigious and not only had gone to court to get appointed his father-in-law's guardian, and put him in a house with a padlocked door, but also had sued his sister-in-law, plus took on a gas station. This gas station charged him for two more gallons of gas than the tank capacity in his car stated. "You overcharged me!" my brother said.

"No, we didn't," they told him.

So he went to court and got them put out of business. Me? I might complain and if that didn't work, I would—in future—not go to that gas station.

And there were malpractice suits, plenty of them. I'm not saying they had anything to do with his medical skills, but a Jew ob-gyn in Alabama is going to be subjected to them. Any time an Alabamian has a baby born without a brain, it's going to happen. My brother has, therefore, become inured to the agonies of our legal system.

My father was so nervous he had Sam removed as executor of his estate. If they took the ice cream and the live-in alleged prostitute away from Veronica's father, surely they would take away Dad's pot.

an attempt at explanation

Okay, none of this is coming out right. I want to try to explain how I ended up living in Schuyler County absolutely dead broke, in the middle of nowhere, and doing nothing but visiting my mother in a nursing home, trying to clean up her house, which has books up to the ceiling in every single room, and going to the emergency room in the middle of the night when the home calls to tell me Mom's fallen out of bed and they have no one to take her to get checked. My writing career's gone to hell in a handbasket, and then there's my kid: she's not happy. It's hard changing schools in eleventh grade.

There's more. It all goes on, the minutiae, the nonliving, while my brother, who's about to retire, is off to Denmark, Hawaii, touring stately homes in England with his wife, and—when he comes up to visit, once a year—berates me about Mom's house not being kept clean. Right. There's mold on the walls because . . . it hasn't been painted in thirty years.

It's all just stuff, I know it. It's all small stuff. I'm not living in a barrio, a tin shack, a favela, a ghetto where there are constant mudslides or shootings. I'm not trying to pick up grains of rice where they have fallen from the back of a truck. But this thought? It doesn't help.

I can't sleep. I can't write. Two weeks ago my horse head-butted me—it was an accident, but still, she gave me a black eye, and I'm starting to think it was worse than that. I have blurry vision and my head still hurts in that spot.

But I keep on going to the nursing home every single day to visit Mom, waiting for the latest attack from my own brother. He started to accuse me of things. Like, my mom's Social Security check is directly deposited into her bank account, out of which I pay my mom's nursing home bills. He's accusing me of committing Social Security fraud. Then I get a letter from him saying I'm embezzling. There's more and more accusations about me stealing Mom's money. He e-mails me vitriol, constantly.

I'm still trying to get Mom calmed down from his visit six months ago, when he went to the home and read James Thurber to her every day for three hours at a stretch. It's become hard for her to talk and she can't move. She was trapped. They had to increase her medication after he left.

And now he's after me. And I am afraid. You can try to be good, you can try to do the right thing, but no good deed goes unpunished, etc. Look at my mother. She was about the most decent, moral, good person on the planet, although she did make a porn film once. It was private and she did it before it was something everybody did, and I don't really see what that has to do with morality. She was just doing what my dad wanted, since he liked girl-on-girl action, just as he loves lawsuits. So does my brother. Lawsuits, I mean: I don't know about girl-on-girl.

divorce in the 1960s

My mom got arrested in 1968, a year after my parents divorced. The local townspeople, had they learned of this, probably would have said it was to be expected. She was already a divorcée, and at that time, in a small New England town, divorce was a shocking thing.

One little girl told me she could no longer come over to play because her mother said I was "from a broken home." In my family, divorce did not just mean Mom and Dad split up—it meant no one else on my father's side ever spoke to us again. Well, except for my grandmother, for a bit, when she came to see my dad. Otherwise, even now, I get these Facebook friend requests from strangers, and it turns out we're related. Their messages are all some version of "I spent a lot of time with your grandmother, who was my great-aunt, when I was growing up—but I never met you, because of the *divorce.*"

At least this makes me realize I'm not making things up.

Dad was busy. He was having an affair with his secretary, and then a bit later with some guy. The secretary lived with us for a while before the divorce—Mom, me, my brother, Dad, and his secretary. Also he was having sex with his patients, neighbors, maybe more guys? I don't know!

It didn't matter to Dad—he had had his tubes tied, or whatever the slang is for a vasectomy.

As he once said to me, "I would never have any more kids, not after the way your mother ruined you and your brother."

He kept the big house. Dad "borrowed" money from his mother, Grandma Anne, although he never repaid her. Later, when he sold that house and could have paid her back, he still did not. "All I want, Julian, is when I get old, you will build a little house for me to live in on your property," she used to beg.

But he never did. And he never gave her back her money. She went on living in her second husband's tiny house in Paterson, New Jersey. It was a step up from the basement she had inhabited for many years, prior to her remarriage. She had spent years working in various discount department stores, where she lovingly purchased for me various women's undergarments of a peculiar nature, and dating a man who was in the Mafia, or who was at least a gangster, with whom she smoked pot even though she did not care for it.

Her neighborhood got worse. Men broke into their house. She heard them coming in the window (her husband, Harry, was deaf). "Harry, take this knife and stab them," she would say. Harry was eighty. The burglars took the knife from Harry and stabbed him first.

There was no use robbing the place, though: it was filled with my grandmother's paintings and items from Korvette's, May's, and S. Klein's—brassieres, sweaters with sequins, and other items you could find on sale.

She and Harry moved to a low-income Jewish ghetto in Florida. Then Harry died, and then she died, and Dad took her ashes and threw them in the wild blueberry bushes on the bank of his swamp and said, "My mother always liked picking blueberries, now she can be part of them forever!" This was at the memorial.

But I'm getting out of order. Mom let Dad keep the big house because she felt sorry for him; Dad loved that house so much he said he would kill himself if he didn't get to stay there.

So he built us, his ex-wife and kids, a tiny house at the bottom floodland of his property. I guess that was part of the divorce settlement. Maybe he just gave her five grand toward it, I don't know. I don't remember the details except at that time Dad earned thirty-six thousand dollars a year and he gave his ex-wife and children five grand a year that got upped to six.

The deal was, he would pay her this six grand a year until we each turned eighteen, and then he would pay her three grand a year for life or until she remarried. But he didn't. He just stopped paying the money.

Going to court with Mom to face off against Dad and his wife was not a whole lot of fun. But who else was going to go with her? And Mom needed the three grand a year! Dad and his wife Gigi showed up stoned and giggling and sneering; and the judge's decision was yes, Mom was entitled to that amount of money. But, still, Dad never paid.

In addition to divorce being such a shocking and terrible thing, there really weren't any jobs for women apart from being secretary or whatever. I mean, when my mom got pregnant with me she had been a dietician, but in those days, you could get fired if you were a woman and got married, or if you got pregnant. My aunt had gotten an advanced graduate degree in economics at Duke, but after that the only job she could get was as secretary to an economist.

People today, especially young women, have no idea how limited the lives of women were back then. They might have let one or two women become doctors—and then it helped if you had connections or were rich—but otherwise, if you were a woman, you were a nurse. Then you married and stayed home.

BEFORE THE DIVORCE, Mom was kept pepped up by a huge permanent supply of some kind of speed, little orange triangles, that Dad got for her by the thousand-pill jar so she could keep her weight down. She didn't have a weight problem, but she had been plump as a child, so it was a constant issue for her. Even if she had been plump, women wore girdles all the time, which was an unbelievable undergarment—thick rubber, tight, hot, and white, with four dangling bands hanging down with rubber and metal clasps on the end to hold up the woman's stockings. All women wore these as soon as you hit about fourteen years old.

If you were female, and a wife in particular, that was just part of the job uniform. In Mom's case it went with getting to live in a beautiful home. Even though she was very frugal, she still had to dress the role of the doctor's wife. The house had Danish modern furniture, the latest in stereo equipment, imported Italian quarry tiles, wall-to-wall carpeting, whatever you could think of. There was an office for his psychiatric practice downstairs, a huge workroom, and sliding doors everywhere; there was an indoor atrium with a fountain and fish pond, a massive fireplace, a huge kitchen with an indoor grill.

But my parents were not happy. Both stalked the halls in the black hole of rage. Both were experts at sulking, but it was not just sulking; it was a cloud of dark hate that could neither be cut through or broached.

There was money, but unless we had guests, the thermostat was kept low, so the house was freezing cold, and winters then were bitter. At that time you could buy monkeys from ads in the back of comic books for twenty dollars, and I got one. The squirrel monkey arrived from Florida in a wooden box. The monkey declined, languishing in the cold, in a cage built by my father. I was afraid of the monkey, since he bit viciously. He was not my friend. We moved him into a bathroom and chained him under the sink, where he occupied his time by stuffing food into the heating vent in the wall.

One day my parents had people over and screams emerged from the bathroom. They had forgotten to tell the guests there was a monkey in there, and while a woman was sitting on the toilet, the monkey had popped out. The monkey was sent to the zoo, where he joined a group of hundreds of other squirrel monkeys who had been ordered from comic books, back when you still could do so.

After the divorce: "Your bedroom here will always be your room," Dad said.

But in the new prefab home I moved to with my brother and my mom, there were cement floors downstairs and no money for anything to put over them. Upstairs there was wood, though. We couldn't afford any furniture, so we had an inflatable couch that did not last long, and a couple of metal folding reclining chairs, which folded up whenever anyone sat down in them and then in slow motion toppled over, spewing out the human contents.

Some nights, Dad came over to our house to screw Mom—not every night, but in between the other women—and then there was a new wife, Annette, but us kids weren't invited to the ceremony because (although his mother was invited) they were going to be dropping acid at the wedding and he didn't think it would be appropriate. Annette was a nurse. Dad explained to me she had sexual frigidity due to having been molested by her brother. Did I need to know that, at twelve years old?

Dad was starting to smoke a lot of pot then; Annette, too.

Naturally, I repeated this to some friend—I hadn't been told not to say anything—and one day when Annette took me shopping she said she had found out I had been telling on them, although she wouldn't tell me who had told her. She said that I was never to repeat this and that unless I kept my mouth shut I was going to get my dad fired and the FBI would take them away.

The shopping wasn't any fun, although it was supposed to be entertaining for me to watch her buying an expensive Marimekko dress and a fifty-dollar white china gravy boat. I guess it was something of a break for me from vacuuming their house and weeding their garden.

Dad was furious. "You bought a one-hundred-dollar dress and a gravy boat? The gravy boat is ugly!" he said to his wife. It didn't matter that it was her own money Annette had spent.

Poor Dad. No wonder after he dropped me off that night at the village fair on the town commons, he went back across the parking lot and got into his car with another woman, who wasn't Annette.

When Annette kept on with her frigidity and bad taste in china service, they went to Mexico for six months so Dad could cure her. I guess it didn't work, though, because when they got back Dad still stopped by to see Mom. She would go out to try to find a new boyfriend, but Dad was right back in there. I think what finally inspired her to leave was my comment, "Dad has a pair of binoculars on his deck, and when I looked through them, I saw they point right to your bedroom!"

You could get trapped in that town and never escape. I had a girlfriend whose parents split up a few years after mine. Her father was a mathematics professor at the University of Massachusetts, but her mother had to get a job as a cafeteria worker in a school so they would have enough money to survive on. When my friend was still in her teens she had a baby.

People think the 1960s was all about being a free spirit and ending repression. They don't realize, there still weren't any real jobs for women, that women felt guilty and ashamed about getting divorced, and that even if you wanted to have an abortion, they weren't legal. The shame and stigma of divorce today is about as well remembered as the feeling of what it was like to wear a girdle.

israel in 1968

Mom was brilliant. She went back to school, got an M.F.A. in poetry, and then got a grant from the Radcliffe Institute to write. Her parents were not well off, but they said they would help pay if we wanted to move to Israel. So, in June of 1968, we rented out the house and left the country.

My brother was not all that happy about going there, so Mom said we would try it for a year and if my brother still wanted to come home, then we would. I was twelve, and my brother was ten.

Our poodle, Fury, was sent up the hill to live with Dad and Annette in the big house. Mom rented out our place, fully furnished, with our three beds on metal frames, the inflatable sofa you had to blow up every time someone sat on it, and our two family heirlooms: a quartz crystal and an amethyst geode my grandfather had given her. It was a good thing we did not have more heirlooms, because the tenant, a wealthy woman named Pinky Astor from New York who wanted to try the rural life for a year, stole the large quartz crystal and amethyst geode when she left. I would still like them back.

Maybe something happened to make her feel entitled to them.

I know my dad might have made a mistake, if he forgot my mom was no longer living there and went down one night. After we got back, before Pinky Astor moved out, I went for a walk with Dad, and Pinky emerged from some bushes and began shouting at him. "You are the white underbelly of America!" she screamed.

I was upset for my dad. I can't possibly imagine what brought this about.

My upbringing in the small New England town was the world as I knew it, and very little had crept in from the larger world. It was still Olde New England, with a town commons where cows grazed; the Lord Jeff Inn; Hastings Stationery, a family business where we got school supplies; a shoe store where a red-haired, partially deaf (two terrifying attributes) man sold velveteen Mary Janes to little girls; a jeweler's; and Augie's Tobacco, with a wooden Indian in front, where you could also buy little jokes and tricks, like a packet of chewing gum with a spring that snapped on the finger of the unsuspecting recipient when the gum was proffered or soap that turned your hands black, and so on.

There was a policeman who stood in the middle of the intersection and directed traffic. One way was the Jones Library, in a stone building, and opposite were the cinema and the only foreign food the town had ever seen—a Chinese takeout that served egg rolls and chow mein.

Emily Dickinson had lived in town, in a big house that was now run-down. It wasn't yet a museum, it was just owned by regular people. When you lived out in the country and you went to town, even though you were just going to the library, you always got dressed up: you didn't wear shorts, you put on a dress and regular sandals or shoes.

As it got closer to the time for us to depart for our time abroad, Mom took me shopping so I could get something to wear on the trip. A few shops had recently started to creep into town with influences from the outside: the Hungry U bagel store and a store called Paraphernalia, where there was an Andy Warhol silk screen—his flowers painting, those vivid flowers on a black background with green grass—in the window. My mother and I both thought it was the most beautiful picture we had ever seen. If we could have found the money to buy it, we would have. It was two hundred dollars, more than the price of a Marimekko dress and a gravy boat.

I am not going to quote what this silk screen would bring at auction today.

In that store we found something really great on sale: a sleeveless paper minidress printed with a gigantic human eye. It came folded up in a little bag.

Other than visiting my grandparents in their fourth-floor apartment in Flushing, Queens, and my other grandmother in her basement apartment in Paterson, New Jersey, I had never been anywhere. The El-Al flight was many hours. In economy, the religious Jewish men also traveling got up every few minutes to pray, davening in the aisles, chitchatting with the other travelers. I had never been anywhere.

The main thing about that plane trip was not that I did not know where we were going, or even why, but that my paper dress was ripping. All night Mom had to keep finding safety pins to try and keep me clad. By the time we landed in Israel and everybody got off and kissed the ground—which confused me, a lot—I was basically naked.

There is a reason the disposable paper dress never lasted as a fashion concept.

We were taken to a waiting station for new immigrants. It was hours before we were processed and then driven with others in a van to Netanya, north of Tel Aviv, where we were left at a hotel that was full. Somehow, eventually, a one-room fourth-floor walk-up was found for us across the street.

For a few days everything was a blur—jet lag, heat, light; the noise at night, the clatter of forks and knives on plates, the foreign language, and the braying of donkeys at midnight and dawn. The beach burned your feet, and flip-flops and the water offered no respite. The sand was so hot that globs of oil and tar that had washed up were melted pools that you could not get off if you stepped in one.

Netanya was a village. Two-story buildings, the beach, cafés, horse-drawn carriages decorated in bells and flowers. It was swarming and beautiful and alien. I was in shock.

My mother wore a pink-and-yellow dress and a pink sun hat into town, carrying a pink handbag. She was stunningly beautiful, although to me incredibly ancient, as she was in her midthirties. The men trailed behind us wherever we went, yelling, "You fock me? Let's fock!" Back in the States, nobody swore. I mean, maybe some construction workers did, but only when they were among each other. I didn't even know what "Let's fock" meant. It wasn't English! I still got the point, but as a come-on, who would go out with someone if that was how he asked you on dates? My mother cried and cried, but not because of the way she was being asked out. It was about my father. "Do you think your father will come back to me? When will he come back?"

I tried to reassure her, "Soon, soon."

The soldier boys and girls in their uniforms were handsome eighteen- to twenty-year-olds, and on the beach there were girls in Jantzen bathing suits with cone-shaped breasts, who were amazingly groomed, with glossy flip hairdos and long, painted fingernails, staring at the boys in their tiny, tight trunks. They played a game with paddles and a hard ball, fast as pumas. These were not my Polish relatives of Paterson, New Jersey. These were not my maternal grandparents' coiffed and lacquered Hungarian friends. It was the first time in my life that I saw there could be Beautiful Jewish People.

When it became apparent we were never going to be transferred from the fourth-floor walk-up annex room, we changed hotels and went to the opposite side of town, to a much larger, newer hotel with an elevator.

Money from my grandparents was being wired to Mom's Israeli bank from the U.S. Each afternoon we walked great distances to the bank to see if the money had arrived. But every day, when we arrived at two, at three, at four—the bank was closed.

In the new hotel we befriended an English family. There was a girl a year or two older than me and another who was sixteen, and then the eldest, who was there with her fiancé, and the parents, from Golders Green. Golders Green, England! Never had a name sounded more exotic to me. They had English accents. The oldest was maybe twenty-three; the middle one, Hilary, was incredibly beautiful and sophisticated; the youngest, Linda, was everything I was not: glamorous, with breasts and hips. Had traveled, knew about men, etc.

My brother had been a picky eater but now suddenly could devour anything; he particularly loved tinned herrings in tomato sauce. I could not eat. The Israeli breakfasts were curious: a buffet of fresh cucumbers and tomatoes and farmer cheese, bread and boiled eggs, and dead cats.

There were millions of cats in Netanya, not like American cats. These were long legged, with long faces, strange and Egyptian looking, and the hotel put out plates of sardines swimming in blue poison and the cats ate the sardines and died behind the breakfast table.

I remember a drunk man on the street had a boxer bitch with eight puppies he was trying to sell, and how I begged and begged for one of these. I whined. I cajoled. I pleaded.

My mother spent all her time crying. She had never been out of the United States before, Israel was a rough and young country, nobody spoke English, and here she was with two kids in a strange land where foreigners kept asking to fock.

Now I was crying all the time, too. She got the English newspaper and saw an ad for miniature poodles. We went by bus to Tel Aviv and to the advertiser's apartment, where we bought a poodle from the woman—the gimpy, catatonic runt of the litter, six or eight weeks old. "At least he seems quiet," my mother sighed. "But remember, dogs are not allowed in the hotel! We have to smuggle him in and keep him hidden!"

Then I had a puppy, but all he did was sleep. What was the point? I might as well have gotten a stuffed animal. I missed my dog from home. I still cried.

One night, Linda, the English girl around my age, and her sister Hilary were going to a club. "Would you like to join us, Tama?" asked Hilary. She was the most perfect and tiny creature on the planet.

"You are inviting her to come with us to the club?" said Linda indignantly. "She doesn't know how to dance."

"Yes I do," I said.

"Do you know how to slow-dance?"

"Of course!" I figured it was the same as any kind of dancing, only more slowly.

At the club a soldier asked me to dance. He clutched me very close and tight. I stepped on his feet. I did not know how to slow-dance and I did not like being pulled so tightly to the soldier and it was scary. I was still only twelve.

After that event, I never have been able to slow-dance. That's really why I got an F in my college ballroom dancing class.

mom's arrest

Israel was only twenty years old at that time. My mom took us to public events where I got to meet people like David Ben-Gurion and Moshe Dayan (who was quite sexy with that eye patch). But I didn't know who either of them was. I didn't even know what being a Jew was, really.

I knew I had Orthodox grandparents on my mother's side, but still, what did that mean? My parents did not keep kosher and I did not understand, because it hadn't been explained to me, that you could not have milk if you had just had meat, unless it was breakfast, when you should never ask for bacon or sausage. Asking for bacon or sausage made Grandpa and Grandma hurt and upset. I always felt awful, but there was no way to know what I would say next to absolutely destroy them. No one ever said what their problem was!

On my dad's side were a bunch of Polish peasants who came over to work in the silk mills in Paterson, New Jersey, around 1904. This side was not like my mom's side. This side denied being Jewish as much as they could, which I guess would work until there were pogroms or someone trying to drag them off to concentration camps.

Swearing in Yiddish that you were an atheist wouldn't have saved my great-great-great-great-grandmother, who must have gotten raped by one of the invading Huns, which is the only reason I can think of for my slightly Asiatic eyes.

Although, knowing my grandmother on my dad's side, my ancestor probably wasn't raped. She probably lured one of the Mongolian horde into her shtetl while Tevye was out fiddling someone on a roof. "Oh, Genghis! Genghis! You look like you're good at fixing things. My husband, forget about it—he's useless. Would you mind taking a look at the hole in here? And I want you to try my gefilte fish."

My mom's parents did come over that year to visit us in Israel, though neither my dad nor anybody from his side did. My grandparents came to visit the following spring, after the small cement-block cottage we were living in by then, on the deserted beachfront of Herzliya Pituach, got flooded out and we moved to a cheap hotel.

But the summer of 1968 was supposed to be sort of an adjustment/vacation time before the fall, when we would move to an ulpan, a center for new immigrants to learn Hebrew and the hora.

The hora! Oh, the hora!

Money still had not arrived in the bank there—due to the fact that, day after day, the bank was always closed. We continued to walk over every day in the heat, only to find the bank closed and a sign in Hebrew, so forget it.

The hotel said they had waited long enough for Mom to pay the bill. My mom told the owners, "Look, I'm sorry we can't pay the bill, but the money was supposed to be wired over to the bank, and the bank is never open! I'm not going anywhere, and if you want you can hang on to my passport and checkbook."

That's pretty much all she had to offer. See, back then, there were no credit cards.

She tried to explain that eventually the bank would have to open and her money would clear. But it was no use. The owners of the hotel said we had to pay up or leave.

We packed everything and went out the front entrance. Even though we hadn't been there long, we had a whole lot of stuff. You couldn't buy much in Israel in those days; my grandparents had told us to bring sheets, towels, cooking utensils—you are New Settlers! Then there was the dog, and the dog needed bowls and other items. And then there were other items my brother and I had deemed necessary to obtain: big heavy clay Arab drums with skin tops that only cost fifty cents; inexpensive goatskin or sheepskin coats that smelled very bad; rocks and ancient artifacts like chunks of Roman glass and clay handles from original Turkish coffee cups, all collected on the beach; small carved wooden sheep made of olive wood, and so on.

The English tourist family we had befriended gathered around us and our twelve trunks. The hotel owners came out, looking ominous. The sleeping poodle (who had been hidden in a bag, since dogs were not allowed in the hotel) jumped out and came to life. He had been in a catatonic stupor. Now he urinated over everything and began running in circles, barking, leaping, and biting. A crowd stopped to watch.

I didn't know why the hotel owners were waiting, grinning eagerly, until the police arrived. It was a trap. They had thrown us out and called the cops. Some were in a car and others were in a Black Maria, or whatever you call a police van in Hebrew. The owners of the hotel began pointing at Mom and shouting at the police. Then a whole lot of hotel guests came out to witness as well. Mom was crying and trying to explain the money was supposed to be in the bank and that she would pay, only the bank was always closed.

In the broiling summer heat of the Mediterranean sun, I, the poodle puppy, and my cute little brother (the same person who would, some fifty years later, work to organize my arrest!) sat on the trunks, surrounded by suitcases and bags, as the police swarmed around.

The police huddled to discuss the situation. Then one officer came forward and took my mother by the arm. She was led to the police wagon and they opened the back and led Mom in. She was wearing the pink-and-yellow sundress and the pink straw sun hat, the matching pink plastic handbag, and strappy multicolored platform sandals. The paddy wagon doors closed behind her and they drove away. My brother and I sat on the steps with all that stuff.

"They're taking her to jail. She skipped out on the bill," said Mrs. Grynaple in a harsh, gleeful voice. "That's the last you will see of her."

psychic studies

My mother was arrested and eventually (okay, later that day) released from prison after the police took her to the bank when it was finally open and discovered the money had in fact been wired into her account.

From the hotel, we next moved to a pension outside Netanya. Two young guys from Greece, in their twenties, were also staying there, briefly, and one of them stepped on my puppy while it was running in the yard. This boy—I think his name was Jacques— broke the dog's leg. I have never been so angry in my life. Believe me, the disdain of a twelve-year-old can be very pure and whole-hearted. It was an accident, but in my opinion, no more idiotic creature existed than a seventeen-year-old Greek man tripping over a poodle and breaking its leg.*

At this time my mother subscribed to *Fate* magazine, and she'd

---

* Some years went by. I was an undergraduate at Barnard College. I was fixed up on a blind date? Met some guy in the student lounge? Anyway, we went out. He was Greek. We got to talking. I said I had lived in Israel. He said

brought the whole collection of back issues with us to Israel. The magazines were full of articles about aliens, UFOs, psychic abilities, how to astral-travel, and stuff like that. She would read aloud articles about peculiar, inexplicable events.

Things happened to people. Someone did a load of laundry and when they opened the dryer, there was part of a Civil War uniform inside. Apparently this dryer was a conduit to another time? This seemed stupid to me.[†]

The other articles in each month's *Fate* were usually about things like a rain of frogs in a small section of the Midwest or a woman who panicked and couldn't get on an airplane because of a bad dream and *that airplane crashed*. The Bermuda Triangle was a big topic. That kind of stuff.

I did not like the magazine. It came, I think, once a month, and then my mom made one of us stand against a white wall while the others had to try to see the big aura around that person and figure out what color it was.

There was always that ad on the back that said to contact the Rosicrucians: YOU MAY HAVE LIVED ON EARTH BEFORE.

I never did meet a Rosicrucian. I thought the Rosicrucians were something Catholic, like Jesuits. You could write to them for the free literature, but I don't know why—I didn't.

---

one summer when he was seventeen he had been in Israel. I said, "Some idiot broke my dog's leg."

"Umm," he said.

This poor guy. I still could not forgive him, and cursing, I left.

[†] Years later, while doing laundry, we did find unusual things in the washer or dryer. There appeared more than once a giant pair of women's underpants that could not possibly ever have belonged to either me or my mom, and another time, a man's tie. At that time I still lived at home; it wasn't like someone had been in the house and I hadn't seen him or her.

From the pension in Netanya, we moved to the ulpan nearby. My mother was studying Hebrew with the other new immigrants. Then, for reasons I no longer remember, we moved to another ulpan, this one in Beersheba, where there was a camel market in the center of town on Wednesdays. Here the new immigrants got into food fights on a nightly basis, arguing over the limitations of one hard-boiled egg or one baked potato for each of us. Pitchers containing water were tipped over others. Tables were knocked down. It was a dangerous place. So was school, where the new immigrant kids from Morocco would spit and beat you up. The day we had to line up and get smallpox injections—a needle as huge as something you'd stick in an elephant, reheated between kids over a bunsen burner—I ran away before it was my turn. Each child ended up with a permanent protrusion, sticking up like a little finger, at the site where the needle was poked. Shortly thereafter, we made another move, this time to a beach shack on a deserted strip of road in Herzliya Pituach.

When that place blew down in a hurricane—or at least became uninhabitable—we moved into a nearby hotel. But the beach cottage was, while it lasted, a fun place. At night in our two rooms, with only one small reading lamp and a small electric heater to keep out the chill, water pouring through the walls when it rained, we would practice automatic writing, where you gently hold a pen on a piece of paper and hope it channels words, or use a Ouija board.

I had grown up with a psychiatrist father who said that acupuncture worked because it was utilized on poor, illiterate peasants who believed in whatever they were told. And my mom, while we lived in Israel, found in a used bookstore all the books by the Tibetan monk Lobsang Rampa, a guy who ended up in the body of some Englishman after reincarnation and was able to remember and write twelve or fifteen volumes about his past life as a Tibetan monk. At age thirteen, once he was almost fully enlightened, another, more senior monk had opened up his third eye.

Apparently all Tibetan monks got this done: a spike poked into the forehead, where that third eye is located, which enabled him to see auras and engage in astral projection. This interested me because, if it was true, how come people just don't go to a doctor to get their third eye opened? And how did Lobsang Rampa end up reincarnated in the body of a British person living in the English countryside, able to recollect every detail of growing up in Tibet and breakfasting on tsampas and entering a lamasery at an early age.

That was a strange year of reading, that year in Israel.

We took the bus from the deserted beach, where we lived in a cottage alongside two other mostly empty cottages, in Herzliya Pituach, into Tel Aviv, maybe a half hour away. There was nothing else there, where we lived: just these three run-down cottages and, across the road, the rusted skeleton of a twenty-story hotel that the builder had never finished because he ran out of money. Nearby was an abandoned munitions factory—it had been burned down or blown up. We were warned not to pick up anything metal, which could be an unexploded grenade or shell. If you dug in the sand you would find scorpions—black and deadly yellow. And on the beach, deserted, bags of drowned kittens washed up. I have never been back, but I think today it's all built up and that little beach cottage, had we had the money to buy it, would be sitting on property worth millions.

I wasn't going to school, either, so the Lobsang Rampa library provided the oddest education you could hope for. Along the way—later, too, it's all mixed now—there was Alan Watts, *Zen in the Art of Archery, Autobiography of a Yogi,* Madame Blavatsky, Ouspensky, Eileen Garrett—who knows?

In Israel we eventually left the cottage on the beach after a bad flood, and my grandparents, my mom's parents, gave us money so we could get into an inexpensive hotel nearby. There we met another British family, the Sharkeys, who were on holiday—and at the end of the year I told my mother I was going to visit them in England. Somehow my mom came up with the money for my trip. She and my brother took a boat back to the States and I flew to England. Mom took me to the airport but couldn't go through security. I was carted away. Because we had entered the country on a "family" passport—I had my own passport now—it showed no record that I had ever entered the country. I don't know when they decided that was okay, but I was taken to the plane. I couldn't see my mom. A woman came and found me on the plane. "I haf seen your muzzer," she said. "I haf seen your muzzer and she was crying and crying. I do not think you will ever see your muzzer again." I was thirteen. (Later, my mom told me she had asked this woman to find me on the plane to tell me she was going to wait outside security and wouldn't leave until my plane took off—and not to worry. But, that's not what the woman told me.) We didn't really know this family particularly well, but Mom wrote to them and they said I was welcome.

I don't remember being scared and I don't remember thinking I was only thirteen. Even though it was Swinging London in 1969, the Sharkeys weren't really part of it. They were just a nice, hip family who lived in Radlett, Hertfordshire. Dave had been the first Jewish boxer in the United Kingdom and was a follower of Gurdjieff. Anne, the mother, took me to Biba to get new clothes. Biba had just opened. I remember being very shocked by the fact that you had to change in a communal dressing room, but my mother had given me a small sum of money to go shopping and I had to try on the clothes. I bought an Empire-waist minidress in a Liberty of

London print, another dress with a shirred front and puff sleeves, and a few other items, like a hat.

(By the time I got back to school in the U.S. that fall, I had outgrown the items, so I never really got to wear them much. And I did not realize that wearing clothing from Biba was not going to be normal in an Amherst regional junior high school in 1969. On the first day, a tiny man came running up to me and said, "Take off that hat at once!"

I laughed merrily. It was a large-brimmed red velour hat made by Madcaps. "Take off that hat and put it in your locker!" shouted the tiny man.

I thought he was the janitor. Besides, there was no rule against hats.)

In London we lunched at Cranks—the first trendy vegetarian restaurant—and Anne's friend Barbara was an editor at *The Ritz*, a kind of English equivalent of Andy Warhol's *Interview*, a newsprint underground paper.

It wasn't until 1976 that I went back for my junior year abroad. I had no money, but because the tuition in London was less than New York, my father paid. By the divorce decree he had to pay; he was supposed to pay for my graduate school, too, but he did not. Because of the cost, I dropped out of the Yale School of Drama (M.F.A. in playwriting) after a year, and it was years before I could pay back the student loans I had incurred.

Around the time I dropped out of grad school, Dad began billing me for my undergraduate education, sending letters stating what he had given me for food when the dining hall was closed on the weekends (he gave me fifteen bucks a weekend) or my annual budget for clothes ($250 a year).

But I didn't pay him back.

portrait of the artist with a young epiphany

Even in high school I wanted to be a writer. By then it was 1970 and my mom, brother, and I were living in Newton, Massachusetts. My mom decided she had to get away from that town of Amherst, Massachusetts, one year after we got back from Israel. She wanted to be near her sister, who lived in a big house in Newton Highlands. My mom found us a one-year sublet—the walk-up apartment of a widowed rabbi who had taken his own family to Israel for a year. It was a pretty bleak place, especially if you have been in the country most of your life. I had been used to the country and was not particularly happy in an urban environment. Newton Center was a grim, built-up area of small shops and apartments.

We survived in near poverty. Although my aunt and uncle had told my mother, after the divorce, that she should return to being a dietician (which is what she had been until she got pregnant with me, when she got fired, which is what happened to women back then), Mom did not want to. Even if she had wanted, she would have had to go back to school to be recertified.

She had already gone back to school and gotten an M.F.A. in poetry. It was a grant from the Radcliffe Institute that partially paid

for our time in Israel. But unsurprisingly, jobs for poets were hard
to find. She taught courses here and there in community colleges
and high schools, which paid almost nothing, so she was forced to
eke out an existence for three on the six grand we got from Dad.
She had moved here to be near her sister, but her sister never called
or called back or came over.

We never ate out or bought new clothes or went to the movies.
Our special treat was buying books with the covers ripped off, for
sale at the drugstore. Sometimes there was enough money to get
a pound of hamburger meat. Then, using a little press with a lid,
we divided the pound of meat into thirds, so that no one got more
or less.

It was hard to visit Dad in his huge house with his freezer full
of gourmet ice cream and his stereo system and dishwasher and
indoor grill, his atrium and indoor fountain and floor-to-ceiling
stone fireplace. Mom had to drive us halfway, then wait in the car,
since he was invariably late. From our place in Newton to Dad's
house was a three-hour ride each way, and at his house you worked.
Vacuuming, mopping, preparing meals, clearing the table, gardening, clearing pathways. We always operated under a low (or high)
level of rage; one never could do a job right or do enough to earn
one's keep or behave in a way Dad liked. One summer I said I
wanted to take a course in etymology at U. Mass, and Dad said I
could live with him and study. When I got there it turned out he
planned for me to pay for summer school myself.

I was fifteen and had neither a job connection nor a mode of
transportation to get to a job, but Dad found an ad in the paper for
jobs in a nightclub that was a former Quonset hut. He drove me
there and left. I applied for a job as "hostess," which of course I did
not get. That's when Dad suggested I enter the wet T-shirt contest,
but I was stubborn and fractious even then.

Without the funding to go to summer school, I returned to Newton and my mother's house. I got a job folding shirts at a discount store in a strip mall. At least there was bus service, albeit erratic.

Initially, the rabbi from whom we were now renting might have been some kind of romantic setup with Mom; I'm not sure. But they met and he took off, leaving some stuff behind in his apartment we now occupied. One day I opened a box. "Ma, what is this?" I asked.

"Oh!" said my mom, who had been brought up as an Orthodox Jew. "Those are the rabbi's phylacteries. His tefillin. Just shut the box and I'll put it away." She was upset that I had found these items. This scared me a great deal. I did not know what phylacteries *were*, but just the sound of it made me realize I had done something wrong. I had opened a box of phylacteries! What the hell were they? To a modern kid you could probably say, "Those are sex toys!" and that kid wouldn't even blanch.

Like I keep saying, though, things were different then. I was maybe fourteen, fifteen, I don't know. Sometime after we moved in, I got—found, acquired, was given—paper panels from a billboard, new, that had never been hung. Each panel was huge. And I unfolded them, one by one, and pinned them on the living room wall. When they were installed they made a picture, a portion of this giant billboard that would have been, I don't know, five stories high on the highway. So now, one end of this living room was taken over by a huge photograph: ONE GIGANTIC EYE. The room of this dreary apartment did not look any better, but it was unusual. That living room now appeared even smaller, covered with part of a billboard of an eye at one end. Design-wise, it didn't really work, but that was my mother, who always let me do whatever I wanted. It was encouraging that I didn't have to follow rules.

Downstairs, there were two doorbells. One was for the downstairs half of the house, the other was for this rabbi's apartment. And I got a little can of red paint and I painted the button of each doorbell. They were matching doorbells, and now they had red nipples.

I'm sure those neighbors didn't like it, but they weren't Jewish and I doubt they had a way to reach the widowed rabbi in Israel. Anyway, what could they have said? "Your tenant's daughter painted the doorbells so now they look like nipples"?

They themselves were pretty rough, anyway; this was not a fine area of Newton, Massachusetts. This was for the people who lived in houses that got turned into apartments. The daughter who was my age spray-painted her name at the bus stop, and this was a long time before graffiti was in art galleries. Back then people who tagged were considered mentally ill or juvenile delinquents.

Ten years later, in New York City, spray-painting became a career choice, but 1970 was the year that the book *Love Story* by Erich Segal was published. That early graffiti tagger was reading it. One night I was downstairs there, and I read it, too. I thought it was a bad book, but I also thought *Catcher in the Rye* was stupid. (How much longer is that book going to remain an American classic, with that pretentious, obnoxious little prick Holden Caulfield dictating some odd version of honesty?) But now I would give anything to have written *Love Story*. Just saying.

The school I went to in Newton was part of a regular public school, but it was separate. It was an experimental school. You were supposed to teach yourself.

Some parts of the experimental concept worked. Not for stuff like math, though, or foreign languages, or science—so basically I missed ninth grade. I had already missed seventh, living in Israel, when I hardly went at all. At Weeks Junior High School—I forget the name of the experimental program—you didn't go to school at all one day a week but were supposed to work at a job that day. It could be volunteer or otherwise.

I found a volunteer job at the zoo, and spent a lot of time shoveling manure and other things. One day, the elephant keeper asked me to watch the baby elephant while she took a lunch break. She handed me a whole bunch of tiny bottles of Johnson's baby oil, the tiny travel-size ones, and told me to give the baby elephant a rubdown. Then she left.

This elephant was young, but already weighed hundreds of pounds and was as tall as me. The skin of the elephant was dry, thick, and bristly. It was in a big round pen and there was a crowd watching. I entered the round pen with the baby elephant. It was a hot day, and I was dressed only in shorts and a tank top. The elephant was naked.

I poured oil on the elephant. Now it was no longer dry but slippery, being massaged by a semi-naked fourteen-year-old. In the sun it was hot. Soon I was covered in oil, too.

The crowd watched with interest, growing in size.

Suddenly the three-hundred-pound baby elephant grinned, backed up, and came at me. It ran into me, slamming me full force with the top of its hot, heavily greased trunk.

Already slinky from spilled baby oil, punched in the stomach at full force, I was thrown up in the air and back, sending me down in front of the audience, which was now howling with laughter.

The wind was knocked out of me. So was any pride I had at being in charge of the baby elephant. I lay flat on my back for a few minutes before I scuttled out of the pen and staggered off.

mom becomes a boardinghouse landlady

How would we survive? Mom wasn't earning any money and Dad was giving us hardly any.

The rabbi was due to return, so we needed a new place to live. My mother answered an ad for a job as a landlady for a house owned by some people in Lexington, Massachusetts. Now retired, the couple who owned the place were joining the Peace Corps, heading to Sierra Leone and leaving behind their dog and their youngest son, who had not yet moved out, along with a bunch of tenants renting rooms in the back half of the house. We moved in before the couple went on their adventure, so they could show us the ropes.

It was a big ramshackle Victorian house in a fancy town. The tenants kept to themselves, except for the owners' son, in his early twenties, who took all his food to his room, where he saved it under the bed. He only came downstairs to clean his guns and rifles at the kitchen table.

Then there was the neighbor. She had been having an affair—for twenty years—with the man who had gone away to Sierra

Leone with his wife. Now lonesome for her boyfriend, and irritated by her own husband, she liked to come over, unannounced, especially when her son returned to live with them, bringing his team of sled dogs.

One day my mom made a very fancy lasagna and left it on the counter. When she came back, it appeared to have been elegantly sliced down the middle. The whole front half was gone. There were various people under suspicion. First was the rifle-cleaning son, who left chicken bones under his bed, followed by the neighbor, who we believed suspected my mom of having an affair with the man who had gone to Sierra Leone with his wife (she wasn't).

Our paranoia grew until one day when we came into the kitchen we discovered that the house dog (we were also looking after him for the year) was able to reach high enough to devour food left on the counter, depending on how close to the edge it was positioned. In a sense this was a bit of a disappointment. Nobody wants to have their paranoia shoved down their throat, not when you can blame a neighbor for sneaking in and eating half your casserole.

The dog's name was Brahms and he was a semi-poodle. He was an early evolutionary prototype of a labradoodle or a goldendoodle, before these hybrids existed, and because of his early stage on the evolutionary scale, he felt no shame about leaning over onto the counter. I am sure later hybrids had more brains, or else this breed would not have survived. But it was too late: once various suspicions have been raised, the enemy is out there.

The couple wasn't going to come back for another year, but my mom hired a new boardinghouse landlord and we moved.

This time it was to a tiny ranch house, still in Lexington, but very much on the wrong side of the highway. Lexington was important to my mother: it was known for its good school system; also, anywhere else was far too expensive for us. She sold the prefab in Amherst and the money got us this place, with a tiny fenced-in front yard and a massive herd of rats occupying the backyard, built on the edge of the highway next to a chemical-scented swamp.

Still, for once, I got to go to the same school for two years. In tenth grade I found a loophole: if I took one specific course, something like American History, I would be allowed to graduate at the end of eleventh grade.

And what did we do in that crummy house for my last year at home, when I was in eleventh grade? Sometimes my mom would drive me and my brother a couple of hours away to a meeting point in a parking lot where my dad would pick us up and take us back to his beautiful home, where there was heat and hot water and we would work for the weekend for food. Or he would get my brother up on the roof there, which was flat, to plant and harvest marijuana. Marijuana was very illegal then and was a big crime to smoke. To grow it was even worse.

Then, after the weekend, we were back with my mom. She was teaching whenever and wherever she could: adult-education classes in poetry at community colleges, or in high schools that had enough money for one "extra" arts class.

When she was out of work, which was often, I would go with her to wait on the unemployment line. It was the time when all the steelworkers were out of work, so that made for an interesting time. The steelworkers were huge, muscular men weighing hundreds of pounds, kindly and tough and from another planet—the planet that we were trying to escape. That planet represented the working class. Now, I am old. I am educated. I have met rich people, including socialites and aristocrats with titles. I am happy with the working class. I do not need to escape their company. Then, however, at fifteen years old, I was in search of upward mobility, though I did not understand it at that time.

At home, what did my mom and I do? At night, at the table, eating tuna fish sandwiches, we read. We read anything and everything. We had stacks of books from the library; we had used books from sales; we had those books you could buy at the drugstore for twenty-five cents apiece missing their covers that came with the threat: DO NOT BUY THIS BOOK IF THE COVER IS MISSING.

Now I don't remember what we read back then. But these are some of my favorite books: *Alice in Wonderland, Papillon, Robinson Crusoe, New Grub Street* by George Gissing, *Down and Out in London and Paris,* and *Down Among the Women* by Fay Weldon. Larry McMurtry. Jean Rhys. *Tracks* by Robyn Davidson. Memoirs by guys who joined the Foreign Legion.

Anybody who's a loser, an idiot, a victim, or engaged in a basic struggle for survival: I'm there. When I read a book I just want a bunch of interesting stuff to happen, adventure-wise, like *In Cold Blood,* without too much musing and thinking and philosophizing.

I don't want a moment of epiphany. I want to go someplace worse, different, more interesting than where I am. So when I stop reading, I can feel good, even if I'm in a cramped economy seat on an overnight flight, or in a filthy kitchen where I should be doing dishes.

london in 1976

I "studied" in London for my junior year of college, from 1975 to 1976. I found a program at Goldsmiths' College, which at that time was not a fancy art school but a teacher-training program. It was the first year the college was trying to attract American kids to study there, so they made a catalog that looked like an American university catalog, offering classes like "The History of England through Furniture, M–W 10–12." But when you got to the class it turned out that it was a group of guys who were learning to make furniture and that day they had gone off at 9 A.M. to visit the chair factory and wouldn't be back until five. Stuff like that.

I had fun, though. One day I was hanging around the Tate Gallery and some guy and his friend started following me. The guy looked kind of like Andy Warhol and it turned out he was from Neptune, New Jersey, and he invited me to his flat for dinner with his wife. She was a stripper in a pub at lunchtime and she encouraged me to work as a stripper there, too. She said the clientele, primarily lorry drivers, was always glad to have new bosoms to look at.

I said my breasts were quite small but she said it didn't matter. I asked what the pay would be and she said four pounds—I think—

for a two-hour shift, and that did not seem like very much money to me, and in addition I still did not want to dance half-naked in front of truck drivers, despite my dad's wish years earlier.

This couple said that for fun we would play strip Monopoly before dessert was served, but I would not have to take my clothes off. So when I lost the round Lyn presented me with a long evening gown to wear, but it did not fit very well at the top.

Then Ted lost his turn and Lyn made him unzip his flies (I don't know why it's plural in the UK) and serve dessert with his penis hanging out.

Then they said it was time to go to the party. This party was quite far by the tube and it was in the loft of a man named Andrew Logan. He lived in an old factory that was full of all the items from the department store Biba, the incarnation after the one I had first gone to in 1969. It had reopened as a splendid department store with a roof garden. But I missed it.

Andrew Logan had things like giant gold palm trees made out of stuffed fabric and plastic hamburgers. Lots of great items from that store were now in this guy's loft.

Nobody was living in a loft then. His was in some odd old factory, way the heck in the middle of nowhere. Later it burned down. I didn't even know who he was or what he did. He reminded me of the Mad Hatter, with a reedy nose, long face, quite manic—he was friendly as I admired all the magical items.

At about one o'clock the Sex Pistols played. I think it was the second time they had ever performed. They were bad.* They knew about three chords, I guess—I didn't know anything about music,

---

* John Lydon mentions this in his book *Anger Is an Energy* and says how the audience didn't like them. I am sorry. The audience did like them. It was me, surly and superior, who didn't. I like them now, though!

but basically if you handed me a guitar and told me to strum it, that's what it would have sounded like. Nor did there seem to be any tune, melody, song, or lyrics. Was it a joke? The crowd of partygoers gathered in front of the mini-stage to watch.

One girl named Jordan wore a rubber dress that had fake fur under the armpits, and there was a man in a beautifully made suit in powder blue with large white polka dots. Later, maybe eight years later, in the clubs in New York City you would see great outfits like these, but not at the time. These were forerunners. I said to the man in the bespoke polka dot suit, "This band is terrible!"

"I know," he shouted. "But they're so bad they are certain to be famous!"

It hurt my ears, and I left the room scowling, and I sat in an overstuffed chair scowling. I was not having any fun. Then, because I was scowling, a lot of photographers came out and started taking my picture. I represented "punk," which was just starting.

Then the group came out on their break after three "songs." It was just me and them in this little area off the kitchen. They were very young. They had a lot of pimples. It was their "photo shoot." I was still sitting. They stood sheepish and pimpled. "All right then," one photographer said. "Can you just go around behind her, kind of in a horseshoe behind the chair?"

They seemed somewhat surprised, but they obliged.

At that time, being American in Britain was of interest. "I always wanted to know," one of the band asked, "would you be so kind as to tell me: What is a 'pastrami sandwich'? What's a Colt .45?"

There had been some American program on television there recently that used those mysterious phrases.

Certainly I wasn't interested in anything to do with the Sex Pistols. They seemed poor, uneducated, grubby. Scrawny. A life of baked beans on toast and chips. A mixture of embarrassed and scared. I had on a silvery satin silk shirt, and I had tied up the bottoms of my jeans with thick pinkish cloth strips from ankle to knee, and I had a pair of pointed, spike-heeled black ankle boots with little fins that flapped down as if the boots had collars. This was not what other American girls were doing on their year abroad.

I always wanted to be a groupie, but there was no way I was going out with any of them, even though they seemed affable enough, even puppy-doggish. But I was hoping to move up on the social scale, or at least out of poverty, and there was no way these guys were ever going to play again, in my opinion, after tonight.

The whole thing was so ridiculous, I started to giggle. After a short while the photographers didn't want to take my picture anymore, because to be punk, you had to scowl. To be punk you were supposed to look disenfranchised, or it wouldn't have any value as a trend.

Somewhere out there are a whole bunch of photos of me with the Sex Pistols. I missed so many opportunities along the way because of my fears and shyness! If only I hadn't thought the Sex Pistols were so untalented and unattractive, I could have ended up as Nancy Spungen.

a side trip to france

Before I left for my junior year abroad, Mom and I both read *Without Stopping*, Paul Bowles's autobiography, in which he wrote about being a young man—about the age I was then—deciding he would become a writer.

So he wrote to a bunch of famous people, inviting himself to stay with them. He did not know the people, but most of them said yes, do come and stay with me. If I got a letter from a stranger, even though I'm not famous, I would *not* invite them to stay with me or even meet them for a cup of coffee. I am scared of people, even the ones I know.

At nineteen, however, this did not stop me from imitating Paul Bowles. I wrote to him in Morocco and suggested he invite me to stay with him. He wrote back, "No."

But others did invite me for lunch, or for drinks. And now I have a great deal of gratitude toward them, for, if I were to receive such a request today, I would not be able to deal with it. I would copy Paul Bowles again and say, "No."

But, on receiving my letter, Lawrence Durrell invited me to visit.

I had read *The Alexandria Quartet,* which I didn't understand, mostly. This was exciting beyond belief, and when I wrote to my mother (we did not have enough money for transatlantic phone calls), she wrote back and said, "Yes, of course you should do this!" She scraped together enough money for me to take a plane from London to Paris, another flight from Paris to Montpellier, and from there to take a bus to Sommières.

I wrote to Mr. Durrell again asking if I could visit soon, as it was my winter break. He didn't answer. Perhaps he had gotten nervous about this lunatic writing and inviting herself to his home in France?

So I gave him one last chance. I wrote to him again and said that I would be arriving on such-and-such a day and that if he did not want me to visit he should let me know, otherwise I would be there.

He did not write back.

I assumed this meant "Yes." Otherwise he would have written back to me saying, "No." Right?

Although I had taken French all the way through high school, when I got to Paris I realized that I could not speak French. Being able to conjugate a verb and knowing vocabulary lists was not enough to communicate. Then there was the whole gender thing that was a killer.

This was a race of people that assigned sex roles to books and plates and ice cubes, and if you didn't get their identity correct you would get an F on the final. Many French people speak English now, but back then, even if they did speak English, they were not going to let *me* know. It was a matter of pride.

In Paris I got another plane. In Montepellier, I left the airport and found a bus. I took that bus for a while and then I got another bus.

How the heck did I do this? I didn't speak French, nobody spoke English, and there wasn't Mapquest or GPS or anything. There were no ATM cards, there were no cell phones. That nineteen-year-old—broke, scared, brave, adventurous—whatever you want to say about her, that person wasn't me. I don't know who took over Tama for that period, but whoever she was, wow.

A bus dumped me out. I walked. I walked. It was getting dark. I don't actually remember how I managed to complete the rest of my travel.

It was evening by the time I arrived. All was gray. Dusty. Wintry. Not cold, but that sad time of the day, of the year. My ancient vinyl suitcase was small yet heavy, and it did not have wheels because in those days *they did not make suitcases with wheels.* On foot—from the bus station across the little bridge and down a winding road to Lawrence Durrell's home.

Yes, it was the correct address.

The house was boarded up. Drifts of dead leaves covered the drive, and the garden was a tangled ruin, untended for a long time. On the huge wooden door was a note scrawled on a stiff white card that said, in French, FOR INQUIRIES GO TO THE AUBERGE AUX COCHONS ROUGES.

Ha! I took the card from the door. I studied for a long time. I opened my French-English dictionary.

An *auberge* was a *traveler's inn* or a *public house* where one might stop for a rest after a long day's journey by *stagecoach* (a *calèche* or *diligence*). *Cochons Rouges—red pigs.*

Going to the Auburge aux Cochons Rouges in darkness, dragging my suitcase, back down the road and over the bridge and then another half mile or more down the lane. There it was: an inn or maybe restaurant, and I went in, holding up my stolen stiff placard from Durrell's house with the nice writing on it.

There was a small desk, I guess for people with reservations, but the place was empty. A woman appeared, surprised. Some of the time, inexplicably, I did speak French. Now I was able to inform her: I had come from London to see Mr. Durrell, who was not at home.

She said Larry was traveling for an extended period.

In that case. *Avez-vous une chambre pour une personne pour la nuit avec une douche?*

She was puzzled. She said, at last, that this was a restaurant, but maybe I could get a bed a few blocks away, and she gave me the address.

This town shut down pretty quick at night. Now there was nothing open. It was winter. The address was a shop, the one remaining shop open. I walked up the small flight of stairs dragging my suitcase. To the left was a waist-high refrigerator. There was a small room going back and in the room, a great many stalwart French peasant-farmer types were standing around arguing. I entered. A stunned silence fell.

This terrified me. These rough men were a depraved lot! What if they were making terrible assumptions about me, that I was an itinerant prostitute wending my way through the small towns and villages of southern France? And even worse, what if they were laughing amongst themselves, saying, "*That* girl thinks she can be a prostitute? Who would want her! *Zut alors! Fiche le camp!*" (My French teacher had told me that meant "hit the road" and that it could be very useful.)

Fortunately, the only other complete French phrases I remembered were about how to get a hotel room, a lesson available in almost all French-instruction books. "Do you have a room with a single bed and a shower?" was finally a very helpful phrase, but not if the answer didn't conform to that in the chapter. The words came fluently, which was kind of a shame, because then it was generally assumed I could speak French. Apparently there were a few rooms upstairs. But now I was starving. I was too afraid to inquire if there was anything to eat. I looked around timidly. I was desperate. And in that waist-high refrigerator by the door, I espied large round local cheeses covered with herbs. Somehow, with the last of my courage, I removed a cheese and I paid for it and then I was shown to my room upstairs.

You gotta remember, I was nineteen years old! In the 1970s there was no French cheese in small-town USA. I hadn't eaten all day, and that big ball of local cheese was the only food for sale in the shop.

My room was clean and quiet, except for the noise from the street just outside, for even though the town was shut for the night, the men who frequented the shop were loud and hung around in front for a long time. Since I was raised to believe that at any min- ute an attacker would burst in, I carefully moved all the furniture in front of the door before I attempted to eat my cheese ball. It had no particular flavor except chalk and dust, with a consistency somewhere between cream cheese and a roll of toilet tissue; it was impossible to swallow. Apparently the cheese ball had been formu- lated out of Elmer's glue, for my esophagus was now pasted shut.

Nor was there anything to drink.

In the morning I went to the bus stop and took the two buses back to the airport. I was ashamed. I was embarrassed. I had trav- eled all that way using my mom's money to go to a small town in the south of France to visit a man who wasn't there.

The plane to Paris was very small. It was crowded with people. This was my only chance. Maybe he—Lawrence Durrell—had ac- tually been hiding out in his house and was now taking a plane to

Paris? I thought so, because opposite me was a man who might be Lawrence Durrell.

I didn't really know what Lawrence Durrell looked like, but I was certain that he was this man. Why he would have been flying to Paris today if he hadn't been at his home the day before did occur to me, but I just assumed that when I had first come to his door he was hiding someplace and had gotten the woman at the auberge to inform any groupies that he was away on a trip.

I could not take my eyes off this man as I tried to will him into saying something to me. If he spoke English I could ask him his name, and somehow, I thought, on meeting me, Lawrence Durrell would see the error of his ways.

I kept looking at him like he was the most handsome creature I had ever seen in my life. He was fat, kind of bald except for gray frizz on the sides, with super ugly glasses and the lower half of a gray beard. It was a short flight, so I had to use all my most seductive powers to get him to speak to me.

At first he seemed nervous, even apprehensive. Then slowly a light flickered in his eyes. Yes, he was indeed a handsome and devastating Casanova kind of guy. He had forgotten how often this happened to him, that nineteen-year-old girls could not stop staring at him with adoration.

At last, he spoke to me. I didn't know what the hell he was talking about. He spoke French! I asked if he spoke English, and he shook his head. Finally, it was time. I asked him: "Monsieur, are *you* Lawrence Durrell?"

"*Quoi?*" He seemed surprised.

What? He wasn't Lawrence Durrell?

With that I let him know what I actually thought of him—again, with the eyes. What a jerk, *zut alors*.

Plus, once we landed in Paris, he had someone who looked like a wife waiting for him, a female version of himself. What a cad. I had half a mind to tell his wife her husband was an old letch, trying to pick up young girls on an airplane.

I got the last available seat on the next plane to London. It was a short flight, and you could sit wherever you wanted. Everyone was very noisy and rowdy, had had quite a lot to drink already, and was dressed in colorful hipper-than-ordinary outfits. I asked someone on line ahead of me what was going on. He explained that a clothing manufacturer's convention had just taken place in Paris, and these were the English press and manufacturers who had come over for the trade fair and fashion shows. The passengers ambled on, all of them trying to find seats next to their buddies. A man took a seat and began gesticulating to his friends to come and sit next to him.

Not so fast, buddy! I was right behind him, and even though I could have kept going, and he really wasn't my type at all, I grinned and took the empty seat beside him.

He was old, very old, maybe thirty-five. He had curly strawberry hair. I had always liked the looks of Harpo Marx, but this guy would not have been my first choice for a pickup. Still, I had to make use of whatever was available. And he was the only man on his own in the near vicinity with an empty seat next to him.

Before he knew what had happened, he was trapped. I did offer to move, but, embarrassed, he said no, it was fine. He was a manufacturer who made cheap clothing for Top Shop, which was at that time cheap but not particularly trendy.

His name was Bartholomew Stubbins. By the time the plane landed he had agreed to give me a ride to my dormitory outside London, although he said, "Would you mind if we stop first at my house so I can check on my dog?" His neighbor had come in to feed and walk the dog over the past few days, but he was anxious to get home to see her.

"What kind of dog do you have?" I said.

"It's a rescue greyhound," he said.

I figured any man with a rescue greyhound was probably not a serial killer. And besides, he knew many people in the crowd emerging from the plane. And he was too pink and hairless, a virtual newborn, to scare me.

"Sure," I said.

Even though Durrell hadn't been home, I was still having adventures. So I went home with that man. He did not want to have sex with me. He wanted to wash my hair for me, in the sink. That was not a problem, if that was what he was into, although, in those days, there were no handheld blow dryers in homes.

See, here's what I mean about times changing. It's like, I saw some stupid Woody Allen movie, set in Paris in the twenties, and there were two guys walking down the street and they were not wearing hats. No. In those days, all men wore hats on the street. If you ever go to a movie set in the 1970s in England and somebody goes to someone's house and the man washes her hair for her, in the sink, and gets out a blow dryer, you'd better just walk out of that movie. It is *wrong*.

That guy, over the next six months, took me on a few dates. He took me to his office, where he had really bad clothing on racks, but to me, it was fabulous expensive clothing, it was new clothing, and after much cajoling he gave me a cheap velvet jacket and a few other items. That's the kind of hustler I was. I really was.

back in london

Back in London, I didn't hang out at World's End, the pub not far from where I did hang out—the Queen's Elm—because everybody told me over and over again not to go there, that it was "too dangerous." I did not know that the Sex Pistols hung out there, I just thought, Oh people keep telling me it is dangerous, I'd better stay away. So I ended up at other places and parties with the same people I had been warned against.

If somebody told me some place was dangerous, I believed them. I was studying abroad on leave from Barnard College, Columbia University, and New York City at that time—at least Morningside Heights near the Barnard campus—really was too dangerous to go into, if you were a young white female. It was the time of *The Panic in Needle Park* and a lot of crazed addicts, and a lot of anger and rage.

Only a couple of years previously, in 1973, I'd ended up at the headquarters of the Black Panthers, up in Harlem, even though the Black Panthers were almost extinct. They were hiding out in some kind of run-down brownstone house probably valued today at five million dollars.

The people who brought me and the other kids attending the National Encampment for Citizenship made sure we "got it": these were some very angry people and it was not safe and we would (if white) probably be killed. But I think by then the remaining Black Panthers weren't all that interested in actually murdering, raping, and shooting a bunch of visiting teens who couldn't even provide any media coverage.

New York City was not London. New York City in the seventies was a lot tougher than London.

But because of things like this, I believed people when they said the World's End pub was far too dangerous for me to go to. I went once, anyway. It was empty. It was an off night, I guess. Nearby, by accident, I stumbled into the Malcolm McLaren–Vivienne Westwood shop called SEX. It was a store, not a bar or political headquarters. In that era, however, it was very embarrassing to go into an establishment called SEX.

I went in by accident. I was walking by. I walked everywhere. I had no money for the bus or tube. I wanted to see London. I saw this shop, I went in. There was a rack with a half dozen T-shirts hanging on it. The shirts said SEX and had big rips and were held together with safety pins and cost sixty pounds. Some I think were eighty pounds. That was a huge amount of money.

See, nobody was doing anything like that and nobody had ever done anything like that, but to me, that was so much money that I could have lived on it for a month. I looked at those T-shirts and I thought, If I want a ripped T-shirt with safety pins I can buy a T-shirt for a pound and I can rip it and I can buy safety pins for twenty-five pence and I can rip it and safety-pin it for £1.25 total.

Of course it would not have the word SEX on it, but why would I want to go around with a T-shirt that said SEX?

I was deeply offended by the price tag and that someone who bought this would have so little imagination they could not make their own. I didn't get the politics of it.

I was doing things like strapping the legs of my blue jeans tighter with thick fabric tape, and I had an alligator bag, kind of like a doctor's bag, that I had bought from another girl for ten pounds. I had a striped sweater with holes and bell-shaped sleeves and I had the pointy boots with spike heels and I had a jumpsuit made of waxed black paper.

It was the same concept as the paper dress that I had worn on the airplane to Israel less than ten years earlier, but it was of heavier paper, coated, and it had a zipper up the front. The only problem with that jumpsuit was the same problem as with all jumpsuits, you had to unzip it to the crotch and basically get undressed before you could pee. But I loved that jumpsuit. I wore it all over London until some people popped out of a shop and I was asked to be a hair model for a show at Vidal Sassoon.

For days the stylists worked on me. They dyed my hair purple and then permed half of it to look like a bunch of grapes. I was told to arrive at a certain day and time at the Royal Albert Hall, where me and other girls who had also had their hair cut and dyed to resemble fruits were placed under a giant sheet with only our heads sticking out and then we were pushed out onto the stage. "You are a fruit basket!" we were told. In the audience were three thousand hairdressers from Japan. I was a model for Vidal Sassoon! With purple hair shaved on one side and permed on the other and my black spike-heeled boots and my jumpsuit or bandaged jeans I was punk, but I did not know other punks as I wandered around London and then Paris.

In those days London was quite a different city; even though it was the seventies you still felt it had not quite gotten over the war; it was so provincial compared to the United States and particularly New York City. The pubs opened only from noon to two and then from seven till eleven, some peculiar hours like that; after eleven, if you wanted to drink you had to be a member of a private club—I wasn't a member, but the frequenters of the Queen's Elm belonged to the Factotum Club and took me with them.

The shops were closed on Sundays and there were few buses and the tubes stopped early. The people lined up politely to get on the buses and there was not much traffic, even on Oxford Street. The only breakfasts you could get were at these horrible cafés with bad coffee and beans on toast, an item that to this day does not, to me, belong at breakfast. In fact, beans on toast doesn't belong at any time.

There weren't malls and giant supermarkets with nice food. The city was gray and grimy and bleak and years behind New York City (aside from the fashion-forward underground). There were a few Indian takeaways, and Soho had Chinese restaurants. Soho was a rough area with a sex trade, I guess, though it did not seem threatening to me, not after New York City, where the rough and dangerous areas were a million times worse.

Homosexuality was illegal. Men could be arrested for dancing together. The drug addicts gathered in Piccadilly Circus and everything was covered with pigeon droppings and television had limited hours of programming and only a couple of stations.

There were shows like *Angels*—which took place in some then-rough part of London, like Islington. The "Angels" were the nurses who worked in the hardcore hospital there, but it was slow—so slow, it was slower than the slowest U.S. soap opera, and I couldn't believe people could watch this show where there was no action and no drama and even the most plebeian statement took forever for a character to utter.

The tubes stopped running by eleven, and after the party at Andrew Logan's I would have been stuck out there. Maybe I stayed until 6 A.M., when the trains started running again. Maybe somebody gave me a lift back to Catford or Deptford or wherever I was living at that time; I moved college dorms a lot.

Some time later Andrew Logan's factory-loft burned down with all those great things from Biba inside. I wished I had one of the large hamburger cloth sculptures, or the golden palm tree. Even photographs of the loft would be great, but this was before people took snapshots of everything all the time. And I did not have a camera.

OH, THE STUFF I DID THAT YEAR, age nineteen. In Paris I was stopped all the time and told I was *"mignon,"* which, with my bad French, took me a while to learn meant "cute." My French was so bad, I thought they kept stopping to tell me about a steak. Most of the men who followed me were very aggressive Algerians. It was some kind of aggressive Algerian period in history. Other times, though, I did meet quite interesting people, like an artist who had me over to his loft to show me what he was working on. He had a bunch of mirrors on the floor and a lot of lemons, which were getting old. His concept was light-years ahead of mainstream art of the time.

So was my opinion of his work.

Other times, I would be invited to parties or asked if I would consent to be photographed or have my portrait painted, or go to a restaurant or club. I was ready for adventure. It came to me.

EVENTUALLY, I HEARD BACK from Lawrence Durrell. He had been out of town and was surprised to learn that I had made a trek to see him. Now he asked me to come there, officially, at a time when he was around.

I went back to the town near Aix-en-Provence and I did stay with Lawrence Durrell. He was sixty-three at the time.

THAT IS A HUGE AGE GAP! I want to say something about sleeping with an old person when you are young. All these old guys who have young wives and think it's because they are so youthful or youthful at heart? It's not. They are either famous or rich. Old guy, you might not think you are old, but you are. To a young person, your skin feels dry and flabby and you smell kind of stale. You get to feel and imagine you are young by sleeping with a younger person with silky skin and sweet breath. (Even a young stinky person is different from an old stinky person.) Old guys can trade in their wives for newer models, but you rarely see old women with younger guys. If it happens, they sure make fun of the situation, like when Liz Taylor had a younger husband who was in construction.

It's creepy and scary if you can imagine being with someone old enough to be your grandfather. Though, come to think of it, I am close to the same age now that Larry was then.

It wasn't his fault. I was just some crazed young woman who wanted to be a writer. I was going to go down to the south of France and absorb the skill or craft or whatever from him. At that time Larry was globally famous. He was a rich and famous successful literary writer of world renown. *The Alexandria Quartet* was highly critically acclaimed and published in just about every language. In fact, he had done so well that we tooled around in a fancy little van his publishers had sent him as a gift!

He lived in a big French house—not a château, by any means, but a large, grand French house with a walled garden. Inside was quite vast; there was a huge bathroom he called "Hollywood" because he had had it redone and it was all glossy red tile and gold and I forget what else. A big kitchen, a greenhouse room, upstairs his study, bedrooms . . . in the garden was a bust of his last wife, who had died of cancer. There was one daughter, about my age, who lived in London, from another marriage.

The first night he took me to the Auberge aux Cochons Rouges and the food was fabulous. After the amazing French dinner, we went back to his house, and believe me there was plenty to drink. I did not know it, but he was pretty much drinking all day long, so I was shown to a bedroom. At 3 A.M. I woke up and there was a presence in the room with me, a presence so strong it actually woke me up. I did not feel frightened; it wasn't a malevolent spirit or anything like that.

At breakfast I said to Larry, "Gee, did somebody die in that room?"

He said, "Do you mean my wife? No, why?"

And I said, "You know, a . . . presence woke me up."

"Was it at three A.M.?" he asked.

I said, "Yes, but it wasn't malevolent."

Apparently a number of other people had slept in that room and the same thing had happened to them.

There were croissants and coffee for breakfast. A couple of hours later he broke out the little mini pizza tarts from the deli—they were delicious—and he offered me a drink. I forget what it was, but he said it was known as "elevenses," which is when we started drinking. I figured it was normal.

He told me lots of anecdotes: all about Henry Miller, who

had been his good friend—they lived opposite one another on the square of some village. In his opinion, Miller stopped writing novels after he began answering people's letters, and he would write these ten-thousand-word letters, which used up all the words in his head.

Larry had stories about T. S. Eliot and Marianne Moore, and how T.S. followed Marianne Moore out someplace and when she came back her cheeks were bright pink and they had "done it together."

We drove around the streets, windy and dangerous and at that time of year, deserted. We visited his future gravesite, which he came to look at quite a lot. He had people over one night; he asked me across the hall to his room . . .

A day or so later he gave me a wad of cash—because he knew I was broke, it wasn't like he was paying me, or paying me off, or anything—and I got on a train to Paris, where I stayed in a small hotel on the Left Bank he had booked. I went to the places he had instructed me to see.

In the morning I arrived by nine at La Coupole and, as instructed, took a seat in the back facing the door. It was pretty empty as I ordered a croissant and café au lait. Sure enough, in came Samuel Beckett, shabby and hawk nosed, sliding into his usual table. A while later Simone de Beauvoir, also facing my direction only a few rows nearer the door than Beckett, took a seat in her massive ratty fur, reading the paper and eating croissants and from time to time looking at me with a certain . . . puzzlement, maybe. And finally, Jean-Paul Sartre. I couldn't believe it. There I was at La Coupole having breakfast next to one of the greatest philosophers of the twentieth century, one of the greatest playwrights, one of the great literary figures—and nobody else was in the place!

And they weren't even speaking to one another. How could this be happening? Could you crowd a room with this kind of brilliance and ever get over it in your whole life?

I wanted to grab life and run with it and be fearless and have adventures and see the world.

new york city, 1977

Back in New York a year later, during my senior year, Studio 54 opened and I went with some others from Barnard and Columbia. Outside was a mob scene, crowds pushing and shoving to get in. I don't want to go in if these are what the people are like outside, I thought. I mean, if you couldn't stand the people on the street, why would you want to be trapped indoors with them?

So I did not go to the opening night, but I did go the next night and a few other times. This was the first time in New York when people gathered around the entrance to a club waiting to be given permission to come in. You went in and it was kind of shabby. There was a long mirrored hallway like an old movie theater (the place had been a television broadcasting studio), then a coat check to one side, and off to the other side were circular bars with very sweaty half-naked bartenders. There was always someone giving you a "free drink ticket." I don't remember ever having to buy a drink there. All the half-naked bartenders were very young, and for many people getting in that club meant entering an oasis of acceptance, something hard to understand now.

I never really liked it. It was so dark, so noisy, and you couldn't see or hear, although there was a giant neon or illuminated moon sculpture that would come down from the ceiling from time to time. This moon was a silhouette of the Man in the Moon holding a coke spoon up to his nose, and the lights would twinkle, indicating the Man in the Moon was inhaling. Then everyone who was dancing screamed. Disco music played over loudspeakers. I remember it as being things by Donna Summer and "The Hustle" and sometimes live acts were up in front—the Village People?—or others who lip-synced to their hits.

You didn't need anybody to dance with, you just got out there and writhed in various lighting conditions, strobe light for a minute or two, then disco ball lighting. Sometimes flurries of snow (soap powder, I don't know) would come down, and you had to be careful when you were dancing because you might slip or somebody could suddenly shove a popper up your nose. I am not sure what these things were. I mean, I know they're amyl nitrate, but if someone stuck this under your nose you got a blast like you had just gone out in subzero weather in the Antarctic, a blast of freezing horror right up the nose and freezing your brain so you staggered around thinking, "What hit me?" This didn't happen to me more than a few times, though, before I learned to avert my nose.

There used to be Benzedrine inhalers that my dad sniffed constantly when I was growing up. At that time they sold tubes of Benzedrine over the counter for people with allergies. I think they cleared out your nose. There is a lot of mention of these benny inhalers in one of Kerouac's books, and in other books I also read that people would take the cotton out of the tube and cook it to get whatever drug was inside in addition to the Benzedrine—some kind of narcotic? Codeine? Whatever. Anyway, Dad sniffed these the whole time I was growing up. Maybe the amyl nitrate was similar. I know people sniffed them at the moment of climax in sex, I guess to make their orgasms more intense.

There was sex taking place all over Studio 54. There were little alcoves and secret closets. There were so many stairs up to various balconies and lounge areas and it wasn't much fun in high heels. In those days there weren't any deadly or incurable diseases from having sex. Mostly boys and men were having sex with boys and men, but there were also men and women. But I averted my eyes if I bumped into any of this taking place.

There were people at the banquettes sitting around talking, people who were famous, but I didn't know them. Andy Warhol, Truman Capote, Rudolf Nureyev, Mick Jagger. In retrospect, it seems amazing they weren't locked up in some VIP room. But then, I don't think anybody really gave it any thought. To me, what difference did it make who they were; even if I met them I wouldn't have been able to hear them and mostly it was too dark to see anyway. One time I was chatting with an attractive Frenchman, or at least we were attempting to talk, and he gestured for me to follow him. We went upstairs where he opened a door to a little room and I followed him in. He shut it.

It was a closet with mops and buckets for all the vomit. He kissed me and then quickly stuck his fingers up my vulva. "Cut it out!" I said. I was twenty.

"You know what?" he said in a French accent. "I find you very boring." He got up and left, shutting the closet door. Fortunately it didn't lock. It was dawn by then and I used my life savings to get a taxi back downtown to my cousin's loft, where I was staying. I didn't have the key, though, and he had locked me out.

I banged and banged on the door, but my cousin must have been asleep. Only his sixty or seventy pets, which included parrots, toucans, cockatoos, hedgehogs, mynah birds, and a peacock, woke up and started to scream.

After an hour trying to get in, knocking on the door, and

pleading, I realized he wasn't going to let me in. So I curled up on the floor outside his door in the hall. I was scared.

There was a book published in 1978 entitled *Disco*. It had a lot of pictures from that time, and there was a big photograph of me dancing with some guy named Sam.

A few years later, in the early eighties, a book came out about graffiti, and there I am in another photo, at the Fun Gallery, surrounded by a gang of kids—Keith Haring, Futura 2000, I forget who else—who are all busy tagging my leather jacket with paint markers. I can't find this book, not right now, or I would include this picture too. I have the book, somewhere. It's buried in one of the boxes.

an influential teacher

My teacher at Barnard, and later at the Columbia M.F.A. program, was Elizabeth Hardwick, one of the founders of *The New York Review of Books.* She came from an era in New York City when literature, books, and the written word were powerful, consuming, important—being a writer or an editor or publisher was something that carried merit and weight in a totally different way than it does now. She was brilliant—married to Robert Lowell, who at that time had left her for Caroline Blackwood and was living in England or Ireland. My mother had taken class with Lowell in Boston. Hardwick was a wonderful teacher, a bit mad-scary as she addressed the woefully inadequate undergraduate women. She brought in and read aloud to us anything that interested her: E. L. Doctorow's *Ragtime,* when it was first given to her in galleys; excerpts from Nijinsky's *Diary.* I knew, even though I was of no importance, her enthusiasm, intelligence, and passion for books were unique.

Her writing, too, was very fine—particularly her eloquent essays—although you could never read one without wondering af-

terward, "What actually is the point?" It was so skillfully done—
she wrote so well without really saying anything, about Henry
James and so many other topics.

She was something of a mentor to me. As an undergrad taking
a writing class with her, I wrote a story, "Maggie, Angel," and she
generously submitted it for publication in the Intro Anthology series, an annual book of winning stories by creative-writing graduate students—I think my story was the only undergraduate work
ever accepted. Her praise, though sparse, meant everything.

She was less of a mentor to me when I took class with her in
graduate school, although she was still more encouraging to me
than others. One student came to her office for a conference. "Now,
wheah did I put your story?" Hardwick said, in her soft, fluty Ken-
tucky drawl. "Wheah can I have put it? Oh, why, heah it is! I put it
in my garbage pail." And she slyly fished it out.

She had me to tea once, in her apartment in the Hotel des Artistes building, on West Sixty-Seventh Street, which was never a
hotel but a unique apartment building above the Café des Artistes.
Over the years I went to a number of apartments there. Each apartment, on entering, had a huge, dark wood-paneled room two stories high, with a staircase that led to a balcony on the second floor,
off which extended bedrooms.

Apart from Elizabeth's, I saw the home of Stuart Pivar, a
friend of Warhol's who was very wealthy from the plastics business
(although everyone said he had invented the Ziploc bag). His place
was decorated with crumbling Jacobean and Italian Renaissance
furniture, heavy red velvet drapes everywhere, like a set from a
Gothic horror movie. There was a gecko who was loose and hid behind the refrigerator, emerging to devour cockroaches. Stuart had
weekly events hosting Julliard music students who played baroque

and classical music, or opera students who sang, but you could never sit down because most of the chairs were too rickety to be of use.

Then there was the apartment of the architect Alan Wanzenberg, who had decorated his residence in dark, heavy mission oak arts-and-crafts furniture, with Andy's former dachshunds and Andy's former boyfriend—Jed Johnson, a designer, who had left Andy for Alan. Jed died tragically in that TWA 800 crash near Fire Island that remains a mysterious accident.

I don't remember so much about Hardwick's décor: I was too in awe of her and her splendid home. It was dark, though. I guess everyone who lived in that building had some kind of need to return to the past. But how remarkable to think that you could, at that time, be a writer and an academic but have enough money to live in such a vast, splendid place!

When I was still at Barnard, Elizabeth was suddenly very happy: Robert Lowell had decided to leave Caroline Blackwood and return to her. This was in 1977. He got off the plane, took a taxi, carrying a painting by Lucian Freud he was going to hang in their apartment; but when she went down to meet him in the cab, she discovered that he had died on route.

Now she's gone too, but I'll never forget what she said about my writing to some publication that did a piece on me. "It's not Chekhov," she told the reporter. "It's Tama Janowitz."

There could be no higher compliment. As much as I adore Chekhov, I would still rather be original.

i was a guest editor at *mademoiselle*

I won the contest to be a guest editor at *Mademoiselle*, like in Sylvia Plath's *The Bell Jar*. Of course, her era was back in the 1950s, and it didn't occur to me that things might be different. The makeovers, the wardrobes given to these women, staying in the Barbizon Hotel, the dinner dances with Yale boys on the roof of the St. Regis—and culminating no doubt in job offers at a magazine.

I bombarded the judges of the competition with as much "extra-credit" material as I could. The only part I remember was an article I wrote called "The Real Ales of England" with photographs of pubs, although I knew nothing about real ale or false ales, whatever they were. I did, however, know a little bit about England since I had spent the previous year there as a student at Goldsmiths' College.

When I won the contest in 1977, it was different. The Barbizon was now somewhat seedy, one of the last of the "residences for women" in New York City where no men were allowed past the lobby, a concept dating back from a time when no respectable single woman would stay in a hotel where there were men. But by then, college boys and girls shared dorm bathrooms. Then, too, several years previously the winners of the competition had complained they didn't get any real work to do at *Mademoiselle,* so we were put to work, which was not something I thought of as part of a prize package.

Living in New York City for four years had already made me somewhat jaded, and I was not so thrilled about going out to see *Annie* on Broadway or receiving a pair of Frye boots, which at that time had not been revamped and were seriously out of style. My hair was chopped off unflatteringly and I was set to work writing an article about bicycle touring in New England, snipping quotes from previous articles and publications.

My four years of college had been spent going to early seminal nightclubs such as Max's Kansas City, in its last days before it shut down; Le Jardin; and the Ice Palace, which, it was said, had caught on fire during a tea dance. I had wandered the city unable to afford the croissants on Madison Avenue.

At *Mademoiselle* in those days Mary Cantwell was one of the top editors, and the guest editor program was co-ed—at the end of our one-month residency the boys went into her office and were offered jobs; at my interview she said nothing, and after looking me up and down for five minutes while I sat, terrified, I was excused.

She was one of the many New York women I met who succeeded by acting utterly cold, superior, and malevolent. I found out that many of them simply were not able to speak. If they did, they sounded like morons, so they had learned over the years to keep their mouths shut and not smile, and, in this manner, managed to seem infinitely powerful. I did not learn intimidation through silence.

In Mary Cantwell's case, I do not know how stupid she was, but she had certainly learned how to intimidate. She went on after her tenure at *Mademoiselle* to write a number of nonfiction books about her life, the highlight or most exciting part of which was her lengthy affair with a married man who did not, ultimately, marry her—and though his name was never mentioned in her books, she later acknowledged that her lover was James Dickey, the alcoholic poet and novelist. This was many years after my time under her aegis at *Mademoiselle*, but I was surprised. The endless description of this love affair with this man she so obviously looked at as a god, who had promised to marry her and who then did not, that was the big thrill of her life? Kind of pathetic, really. And surprising that she ended up being just another woman gushing on and on about some idiot married guy who dumped her. If you had told me while I was trembling in her office that here was a woman who went home and prettied herself up for some drunk poet who might or might not be in town, and if in town might or might not stop over, I wouldn't have believed it.

While guest editor, I was switched from the travel department to beauty and sent to work on a photo shoot. The article was about some young, married, attractive woman who lived in an apartment off Third Avenue, I think. Now, I realize it was just a decent apartment, but at that time I was overwhelmed that people could be so beautiful and live in such luxurious surroundings, and I stood in amazement until I was commanded by someone there to iron a blouse the woman was to wear in her next shot.

It was a lovely white satin blouse, much nicer than anything I had ever had or seen.

"Is the blouse ironed yet?" someone said.

But I had rested the iron facedown on the blouse and burned the sleeve off. I just stood there in shock. I had been sent out on assignment and had just totally destroyed this expensive blouse, and the woman—with her lovely apartment and her good looks and whatever else she had—now had nothing to wear and I was going to be held responsible for it.

They found me standing over the ironing board sobbing and apologizing. There were gasps of horror and sighs of disgust.

A small conference of editor and stylist and photographer and whoever else was there gathered to see what was going on. "Wait here," they said to me, and went to another room.

A beautiful young man with a shock of blond hair came in. He was the hairstylist. "What's going on?" he said. "Why are you crying?"

"I was told to iron a blouse and I burned it," I said.

He picked it up from the ironing board. It was now a shirt for a one-armed person. "You burned this?" I nodded, crying. "You burned a blouse and you're crying?" He had a Dutch accent. He began howling with laughter. I was furious. How cold, how callous. Here I was, utterly devastated. I had committed this terrible act; I had burned a blouse with a sixty-dollar price tag I would never be able to repay. My life was as ruined as the blouse.

Would this have happened to Sylvia Plath? She had been a guest editor and went to dance with Yale men on the roof of the St. Regis hotel during her time at the magazine. There was no mention in *The Bell Jar* of being sent out to iron. But if she had been, she would have ironed beautifully, I am sure. My life and any future career possibility were over.

An editor returned and handed me an envelope. "Please take this back to the office and deliver it."

At least I now had something to do. In shame, sticky with tears, I went back to the Condé Nast building and went to my editor. "What are you doing back?" she said.

"I . . . I was told to come back and deliver this to you," I said, and I gave her the envelope. She opened it. There was nothing inside.

Mademoiselle was a great magazine for a long time. It was directed at college-age women, who were called co-eds back then, which meant, kind of, something voluptuous and dumb, who maybe were taking home economics, but eventually, things changed.

This magazine published many fine articles, some with real substance. It published fiction by Carson McCullers, Truman Capote, William Faulkner, Tennessee Williams, James Baldwin, Flannery O'Connor, Paul Bowles, Jane Bowles, and many others.

Some years later it was brought down by yet another brittle, superior woman, this time English—one of the editors Si Newhouse brought over during that time in New York history when a British accent was a gold ticket to a job.

I had known her, socially, for a long time—but as soon as she got her position of power, she was horrifically rude to me. And, almost single-handedly, she made a fine magazine—which had a niche, a real market audience—into a piece of pulp. And the magazine was terminated.

The damage these Brits did out of stupidity and snobbery during their reign of terror in New York City publishing was horrendous. The British accent was entrée into publishing, magazines, the art world. For magazines it was a bit peculiar, though, because if you ever picked up a British magazine at that time, they were basically unreadable. They didn't make any sense. American magazines were light-years ahead of what they were publishing over there, but the USA still handed over the colonies of magazines to the Brits. Brits came and took over the magazines of America, which began to fizzle and sputter.

Maybe it would have happened anyway.

looking for work

After my graduation, after my guest editorship, I applied for a job at the Condé Nast magazines. Everyone who ever did this after having a guest editorship was pretty much always offered a job, even if only a miserable entry-level position.

Weeks went by and I was back home in Mom's bleak little tract house by the interstate highway outside of Boston. I was still upset about the blouse.

My mother was indignant that my job had been to iron. "You've never been able to iron!" But she suggested I write a letter to the editor apologizing and explaining how this terrible incident had occurred. We wrote it together. It started out reasonably, and then, as the two of us perfected it, became a masterpiece easily equal to Eudora Welty's short story "Why I Live at the P.O."

Now *this* was a letter. If you ever want to know what it was like to have fun, it was my mom and me writing this letter. Writing things like "Well, 'nuff said." Could three words be more supremely irritating? Could three words be more wrong?

July 1st, 1977

Dear Mrs. Berg,

I'm writing to apologize for the terrible thing I did. I have not been able to sleep since I burned that expensive and beautiful blouse. You can't imagine how I feel. I am so tired of being so inept. It is not easy for me to think positively under the circumstances or to be my own best friend. I don't understand how it could have happened. I am usually a pretty good ironer. Well all I can do is try and forget about it, and I would hope that you too will be able to forget and forgive, although perhaps forgive is asking too much under the circumstances. Would I be able to forgive me in a similar situation? I cannot answer that. Such a beautiful blouse!

Well, 'nuff said. Of course, thinking about it, maybe there was something wrong with that iron, since such a thing has never happened to me before. And I was rather tired and weak, since I hadn't eaten lunch, which you said we were all going to go out for together. But when I arrived at the apartment no one was there and I had to wait and wait without any food in my stomach, which made me susceptible to accidents. Actually it was lucky nothing worse happened, because I get very upset when people make promises they don't keep. And what if something had happened to me? New blouses can be bought but I am not replaceable. Nor are damaged feelings easily repaired. How do you think it felt to me sitting there doing nothing but watch that girl being photographed, simpering away as if she were really it instead of a mere nobody whom nobody has ever heard of. And those wretched people, like the photographer who kept saying he would see me again soon and who never called me. I am not using any of these examples as excuses, but merely as explanation.

Wishing you the best,
your former Beauty Guest Editor

Tama Janowitz

Tama Janowitz

If you write a letter like that, it's letter-as-performance-art.

I sent the letter to the editor and my mother and I eagerly awaited a response.

There was none, nor was I offered a job at Condé Nast.

A few years later, I found myself back in that building on my same old floor. Many faces were the same. Some kept a wide berth. Finally an editor did stop by briefly and asked, "Aren't you the one who wrote The Letter?" Her eyes widened with fear as she scuttled off down the hall.

WHEN I DIDN'T GET A JOB with a New York magazine, I moved home to my mom's tiny house on the side of the eight-lane highway and started applying for work.

I had always thought I should go into advertising. It seemed to me that this was a very legitimate and honest form of writing. Because what you did there, as a writer, was to try and sell a product. You were not pretending otherwise. You were not making bad art or literature under the guise that you were an Artist. You were doing a job, a real working job, that sold a product. You were earning a living, and you were doing something somewhat creative, but you were not pretending it was for any other reason than to sell something. Since my mom and I lived alone together, we read and read and had very pure, isolated ideas about Art and Writing. So much had been published, which, in its day, was touted as being great, but wasn't. And the books and works of art that were, in their time, given great critical acclaim and praise ended up being—to us, anyway, really bad. I'm not talking about *Catcher in the Rye*, which had always seemed pretty stupid to us. I'm talking about *Raintree County* and *By Love Possessed, Boston Adventure, Look Homeward, Angel* and *Ulysses,* and an entire first two-thirds of the twentieth century dominated by male writers who were actually pretty lousy but about whom you weren't allowed to say anything.

At least in advertising I would be avoiding this preposterous court of idiocy. So I put together a portfolio of copywriting and illustrated it. I included a lot of things I had done in college, like playbills for a theater group. And . . . I got an interview! This was a big deal, actually getting an interview for a job. I needed this opportunity.

I believed that I was interviewing for a position as a copywriter. The ad agency, however, thought I was there to interview for a position as a receptionist in the accounting department. I don't know how this discrepancy arose, but I did know it was a good idea to dress up for an interview. So I put on my black spike-heeled boots and a suede mini-skirt and other punk items I had gotten in England the year before that had not yet reached the fashion shore of Boston and I strutted into that interview.

Because of the drawings that illustrated my copy, they called and hired me as assistant art director. Now that I was hired, I decided that as a working girl my costume should be a plaid kilt, brogues, a button-down shirt, and a cardigan.

On my first day of the job, everyone gathered around to greet me. Except for women in subsidiary positions, only men worked there. But as I resembled a 1950s schoolgirl, I was not the person they expected. Immediately, all my confidence vanished. The person they were waiting for was, I think, in retrospect, a dominatrix.

I was sent to a remote office and assigned various tasks. My first assignment was to draw a storyboard with a cowboy resembling John Wayne who walks into a bar and orders a can of Underwood Deviled Ham. I could not do this. First I had to find out what a storyboard was. Once I found out, I went to the library every night and traced pictures of cowboys and then tried to draw cowboys, and even if I could draw a cowboy from one angle I could not draw the same cowboy from a different angle. Night after night, I cried and cried.

At the end of the first week I was called into the conference room. "Are you ready to present your Cowboy Ordering Underwood Deviled Ham in a Bar?"

I held up my grimy five-foot-tall storyboard. The members of the ad team and the rest of the account executives looked at it for a long time and then said politely, "Thank you."

Then they sent me back to my office.

They tried to find other things for me to do. My boss asked me to reframe some pictures for him by taking the pictures out of the frames and turning the mattes backward and putting them back in the frames, but when he came to collect them at the end of the day I was sitting on the floor crying and the pictures were ruined.

After that, they left me alone. A month or so later there was a new hire at the agency. Her name was Valerie. She was lovely.

The agency was really trying to make things equal, where women would be hired as well as men!

Valerie and I went out to lunch. "So, Tama, what is it you *do* exactly at the agency?" she asked.

"Valerie, I don't know how to answer that. I don't know. I don't exactly *do* anything here. People have tried to find things for me to do, but thus far, I come here every day and I get a paycheck."

After lunch, she told me she had a meeting with our boss.

After her meeting, I was laid off.

I would never be able to work in an office, or anywhere, I knew that now. With the stressful life I had led until that time, and the constant fear of poverty, truly, I would have been content with any job, a job with a paycheck, benefits, comradeship. But it was not to be.

transgender
publishing outing

I went back to school. I found a one-year master's degree program that offered a full scholarship plus a little money to live on at Hollins College, a lovely women's college in Virginia that predated the Civil War.

It harkened back to an earlier era, to that time when women of fine backgrounds went to finishing school to be finished. In 1978 it was an undergraduate college that primarily consisted of women who brought their own horses and Mercedes. But twelve young men and women had been accepted into a new graduate creative writing program.

At Hollins, I wrote my first book, *American Dad*.

I was taking an independent study, but when I handed in what I had been working on my teacher couldn't be bothered to read it. I begged him, but he was disgruntled and didn't want to take the time. What would become of me? Could I write? And what should I do with this book? I didn't know what to do.

There was a visiting professor, William Goyen, who was helpful and kind and gave me the names of two editors at publishing houses. Six months after sending the manuscript to them, one sent it back. The other said she would publish it. She had me rewrite and rewrite and revise. She said if I did what she wanted, she would definitely publish it. After a year of rewriting she called and said, "It did not pass the editorial meeting. Sorry."

I put it back, pretty much, to the way I wanted it. I sent out sections of this book to different magazines. I sent chapters to *Esquire* and *The Paris Review*. They were rejected.

The manuscript was written in the first-person point of view of a boy. I decided I would take those same chapters and send them out with a man's name on them. I decided to call myself Tom A. Janowitz.

This time the work received a different response. A woman editor at *Esquire* wrote to me: "I really like what you are doing here, Tom. It's not quite ready yet, but I think I can help. We can work together. If you are in New York City, how about I take you to lunch?"

I was too chicken. Her letter was a little flirtier than what I have described above.

Simultaneously, letters from *Who's Who of American Authors* used to come in for my mom.

RESPOND NOW TO BE INCLUDED IN OUR LATEST EDITION, AVAILABLE FOR SPECIAL DISCOUNT RATE $79 TO PURCHASE BUT YOU WILL BE INCLUDED ANYWAY.

My mom always responded, hoping her being listed might lead to something, even though we didn't have the money to buy the actual product. This time, we decided she should—and did—write on her bio that she was the mother *of two sons*. We were trying to prove that maybe things hadn't changed that much since the Brontë sisters wrote under pseudonyms, men's names. Currer Bell got published. George Eliot got published. George Sand.

The phone rang. "Hi, could I speak to Tom?"

"Tom, it's for you," my mother said.

I picked up the phone. "This is *The Paris Review*. We are calling you to tell you we have accepted your story."

"What? Really?"

"Tom?"

"Yes. Well . . . actually."

"I thought you were the author?"

"I am."

"Oh . . ."

The editor sounded disappointed not to have discovered a young male writer, but Tom finally had his first work accepted! By *The Paris Review*, no less.

Months went by, but my excerpt did not appear in the magazine. A year went by. And I was broke and they were going to pay me $150. I contacted the editors there. "I hope you will soon publish my piece; it would mean so much to me to have the book from which this excerpt was taken include this fantastic credit." (I had finally found a publisher but still hadn't gotten paid the small advance.)

"In that case we can't publish your piece," George Plimpton said. "We don't publish pieces that have been published elsewhere."

"Please!" I said. "It's been a couple of years, can't you squeeze it into the magazine before the book comes out?"

My mom called him, begging him and saying how upset I was. It was that prestigious to get into *The Paris Review*. At the last minute they did publish that excerpt. And after I begged for another year or so I did get my $150. But, apparently as punishment for begging, I never did get invited to one of Plimpton's literary soirees. And when he asked me to read at a fundraiser anniversary, although all the other speakers (all men) got to read from their own work that had been published in *The Paris Review*, I was made to read a poem by someone else—a bad poem.

A few months before *American Dad* was published, the editor and the publicist asked me who I would like to have "blurb" my book. So I gave them a list of every author I admired or who might help by writing something about a first novel by a young author.

After a few weeks went by they asked me if I had gotten any of the blurbs.

"But . . . you expected *me* to get the blurbs? You asked me for a list of who I wanted—I don't know where these people live or anything."

"Oh. Well, I'll find you the addresses," said the publicist. "I'm too busy, though. *You* write to them and, um, you can sign *my* name and give my number, then they'll write back to me if they are interested and I will send them the galleys."

I was very discouraged at the thought of having to write to these people, nor did I know what to say, but I sent out a couple dozen letters. Then I took it a step further. Since the publicist was too busy, I would assist by sending out letters to reviewers at newspapers and magazines, again with her name and address.

A short time later, the phone rang.

It was my agent. "You are going to prison," she said. "You signed the publicist's name to a bunch of letters! You have committed forgery. She is very upset. It will be all I can do to prevent her from pressing charges."

"Huh?" I was petrified. "But . . . but she told me to write to authors I admired and sign her name!"

"Not to reviewers, though."

I was twenty-three and extremely frightened. Since that time I have lived under fear of having to do jail time. I am not kidding.

I still think I am going to go to jail at some point, though it won't be Tom but Tama.

Right before publication of *American Dad*, the editor at Putnam's chickened out and insisted I publish under my real name. And so I was stripped of my manhood.

American Dad was published in 1981. But because a cookbook author who was assigned to review it in the *New York Times Book Review* decided to trash it and crush the twenty-three-year-old first-time author, it only sold fifteen hundred copies. Publishers did not want to publish my next novel, nor the next, nor the next. I started writing short stories. It didn't take as long to write them or to get them rejected. My mom was encouraging and supportive as always. She never said, "Go back to school and become a lawyer." She never said, "Go get married." She drove me to the post office so I could mail my stories to small literary magazines. Some days I mailed five stories to different places. Each had to be weighed while my mom waited in the car.

Every day she drove me to the smallest post office. Then the postal clerk said, "You are mailing too many things! You can only mail one envelope a day!"

"What?" I said.

When I got home I called the central post office. "Is it true you can only mail one manila envelope per day?"

"No, of course not," they said. But it still didn't do any good. The clerk in the small post office had his own rules.

Mailing one story a day slowed me down almost as much as writing a whole book and waiting to get it rejected. But I kept at it. And finally, *The New Yorker* published "The Slaves in New York," and everything changed for me.

I moved to New York and found a meat locker measuring ten by thirteen feet that had been converted to an apartment. But I was able to get my second book, *Slaves of New York,* published in 1986. I appeared on the cover of *New York* magazine in an evening dress standing next to meat in a meat locker next to my apartment in the Meatpacking District.

At the time the area was a working neighborhood. It was full of transgendered and gay prostitutes working the streets at night before the deliveries of meat were made at six in the morning. The city was so different then. I would not have guessed that this area—with its hard-core gay sex clubs, the Anvil and the Mineshaft, where men darted down these holes from which bellowed the stench of amyl nitrate and sex, and even after the streets were cleaned there were still bits of skin and gristle and fat from the meat being carved up during the day—would turn into an area with fine hotels where corporations gave parties and events and there were photography studios and expensive shops.

TEN YEARS AFTER THIS INITIAL bout of success, a man named Kurt telephoned me. "I'm calling to say that I know you are really a man. And if you don't confess, I am going to tell everyone."

"None of your business," I said.

"You better tell me the truth!"

"I won't," I said.

"Then I am going to call your dad and I am going to make him tell me the truth."

I called my father right away. "Dad, Dad! There's an angry man and he is going to call you and make you tell him whether I am male or female."

"Huh?"

"Dad! Please don't tell him! It's not his business what genitals I was born with. It's no different than forcing someone to wear the

Yellow Star of Judea on their sleeves. Unless he, she, or it wants to be public, I don't see what business it is of anyone else's."*

So when the person called to interrogate my father, Dad was loyal and didn't reveal the truth. But the man pursued. He grew angry with Dad, who would not discuss what genitalia I had at birth.

So the man put out a kind of newsletter with his proof. His proof that I had been born a man was, 1. I had published excerpts of my first book under the name Tom A. Janowitz, and 2. In some kind of directory of American authors my mom had put down that she had two sons.

The man sent this newsletter "outing" me to all kinds of media. I got a call from *People* magazine asking if I would write an article. I said I would, but it would be about this bizarre person haranguing me, not about my genitals.

People said, no, they only wanted a factual article about my gender. I was against "outing" people regarding their sexual or gender orientation.

This was the nineties, and I thought, Yes, the world would be a better place if people were honest and open—but they should not be *forced* into the open. If you were some sixty-year-old who either had to live all your life in secrecy or be shamed publicly and lose your job and be disowned by your parents, I leave it up to

---

* Recently a group of students from Hampshire College, near my father's house, came on a field trip to view his swamp and artworks. As every student walked in the door, each told Dad their name and announced whether they were He, She, or It, and their sexual orientation. Dad was eighty-six. Both my dad and I agreed: Who cares? But I say this now to show you how times have changed from when my grandmother Lillian would come to visit and hide any visible boxes of tampons in the bathroom in shame and horror.

him—or her—if they want to be public about it. The only thing I ever thought was wrong was sexual relations with children or animals.

Do I want to see a man's penis in the bathroom? Not unless it is tucked under a skirt and he can sit nicely on the toilet with the door closed.

once i was brave

wrote the first story in *Slaves of New York*, "Modern Saint #271," in 1979. Nobody then used the word *penis* except perhaps for doctors. The word had amazing shock value. It is so hard to believe that now. It was not until many years later that the president's penis was mentioned repeatedly in the media.

I wrote that story at Hollins College in Virginia while I was getting my master's. George Garrett came down to give a reading; he had published a story of mine in *Intro 8*, "The Liar's Craft," and he was editing an issue of *Ploughshares* and looking for submissions. I gave him "Modern Saint #271" and he sent it back right quick, with the suggestion I not publish it. He did not want the story and then nobody wanted the story, until I told some kids in New York City who were publishing a photocopied magazine, *New York/Berlin*, in the early eighties that they should publish it because I could credit their magazine in my book when it came out. So they agreed. It wasn't that they *wanted* my story, but they agreed to publish it.

By then I was starting to publish in *The New Yorker* and I was asked to be part of a group reading at Symphony Space. I decided I would read "Modern Saint #271" and another story, "Sun Poisoning." I was next to last, the least coveted position, and I was anxious through the entire event.

You can't explain to people, when you are writing about the past, how taboo things were then when the later generations would not have any issue or thought about that taboo. Did Robinson Crusoe take a crap? Did Anna Karenina get her period? What happened to the guy in *The Sun Also Rises* that he couldn't get it up? I mean, nowadays you would expect to read if the whole thing was gone, leaving a hole that could be turned into a vagina. But the original readers of those books dare not ask, and now it is too late to demand answers from the writers.

Where are the bathrooms and toilets of yesteryear? Charles Dickens, Stephen Crane, Dostoyevsky: Where are the outhouses? Did your character never need the chamber pot? And all those women—no matter how cold it was—only wore dresses. Was there not one woman, ever, who put on a pair of pants?

Times changed. Still, I cannot reiterate just how shocking that word *penis* was. So finally I stood up and I started: "After I became a prostitute I had to deal with penises of every imaginable shape and size."

I mean, that would kind of be the main thing, wouldn't it, if you were a prostitute? That's what you would be dealing with.

Out in the audience there was a sharp intake of air, which was not dissimilar to the way I felt at that moment, like all the oxygen was sucked out of my lungs—and then they began to laugh. First nervous, embarrassed titters, and then guffaws. It was unbelievable, I had that tired audience who had listened to the previous three readers with their nice dozy droning work and suddenly I got up and it was like throwing a bucket of water on everybody. Ice-cold water. They woke up, they were alive, my story was alive.

But times are so different now; you couldn't find a single word to do what I did in that story. Just because everybody says *fuck* and *shit* all the time doesn't give these words any power; it strips the power. The same as you could use the word *like*. As in, "Like, why don't you, like, shut the fuck up?"

I have heard whole conversations on the streets:

"No shit! Are you shittin' me? I mean, like what the fucking fuck?"

"Shit, yeah! That fucking little shit, he couldn't fucking believe that shit."

On the one hand it is just people mumbling and on the other what is coming out of their mouths is feces. And for years after I wrote that story that had the word *penis* in the first sentence, I could not be introduced to any man without his leering lasciviously and discussing it.

I would say, "What I was trying to do was to objectify male body parts the way men have always done about women." But the men who leered never listened. They wanted to think of me as some nymphomaniac, I guess, obsessed with guys' dicks.

After this story, well, immediately another woman published a collection with the word *penis* in the first line; one woman decided to write about women's vaginas, and a kid made a movie where there was a girl writer who wrote about graphic sex and penises for shock value or to get attention. The president had a penis all of a sudden. *The New Yorker* published stories with the words *fuck* and *shit* and books were published with the word *fuck* in the title and so on and so forth.

on lou reed

I knew Lou from a boyfriend who had danced with a whip with the Velvet Underground when they performed, although that was years prior to when I was with him. Now Ronnie was not really friends with Lou; he knew him through the Program.

At that time, in the early eighties, everybody met everybody through the Program. That was a phase when it was so totally hip and social in New York City.

Alcoholics Anonymous, Narcotics Anonymous, these meetings—the right ones—were just as much of a scene as a nightclub. In New York City there were meetings every single hour of the day, in every single neighborhood. People knew which ones their friends attended and that's where they would be, then get a cup of coffee afterward or go for a drink or get some drugs. It was a big social support network. Drag queens, rock stars, artists—people had "sponsors" who they could call day or night to get backup assurance or other things.

Most people in the program still drank. They still did drugs. But when they went to AA meetings they could say that they were sober: for a day, or whatever length of time. Then the people bonded. "Oh my gosh! Congratulations! You've been sober for seven hours!"

I am sure there are still just as many meetings going on in New York today, but I don't think there will ever be another time in history when you'll find so many funky, funny, brilliant, and quirky people all in the same room like that. Because New York City just isn't the same. There are no cheap apartments, like there are no more misfits; back then, if you were homosexual you came from your small town to find acceptance, and if you were an artist, you could afford it, whatever. So Lou and Ronnie were not really friends, even though Ronnie thought they were, but Lou just tolerated him. Nevertheless, around 1983 I met Lou's wife, Sylvia, while she was writing her thesis and hit it off with her.

I went to their apartment. They lived on the Upper West Side in a new building, one of those fancier buildings, but still a small apartment. I think it had two small bedrooms, a kitchenette, and a living room, and was done up in brown—brown fixtures, brown wall-to-wall, and brown sofas. It wasn't how I was used to living and it wasn't like the funky places of most people I knew, who were in fifth-floor walk-ups decorated with the things you could still find on the street back then: old alligator hides on the wall like Cookie Mueller had, or those art deco pieces that were discarded from people who had died. The only thing to me that made the inhabitants seem reasonable was their collection of dachshunds. Approximately three of them, I think, had broken their backs and hobbled around. The other two, Sylvia complained, urinated on her in bed out of jealousy.

It was nice to have Sylvia as a friend, except she would take me to her closet and show me all her new high-heeled shoes, and I am telling you, when you are so poor, it is a hard thing to have someone your age show you their fancy clothing and nice shoes and a rock-star husband playing early electronic games with a red joystick in the other room.

Still, although they had that type of a setup, Lou was not rich. How could he be? The Velvet Underground was really not popular; I mean, it was not mainstream music. If you went out with Lou, say, to a movie, you could be sitting next to him and someone would tap him on the shoulder and go, "Wow, you're Lou Reed!" but that was about as much as he was recognized. And even at that I was surprised: How could someone know—sitting behind him!—that he was Lou Reed?

Lou's country house was about an hour and a half outside the city, in Blairstown, New Jersey, and it had been an old Boy Scout camp, something like that. We went there one day. There was a big fence and you drove down the long lane past a pond. The house was massive, stone, built in the beginning of the 1900s or maybe later, with a huge great room and then these quirky little sleeping rooms off the main area, which had a pool table and a big chandelier made out of antlers. The entire house was dark, and the only place that got light was this bedroom Lou had put on in the back, a more modern glass addition.

We all just sat outside and chatted. Lou was easy to talk to, and he told me about getting electroshock treatment and what that was like, and how his mother had basically forced this on him. He said to me, "After that, a part of me died." And you could see that some part of him really wasn't there.

And he knew I had published one book, *American Dad,* and he talked about his friend Liz Swados, who had just published a book. I think they had been at university together. I was jealous of her, even though Elizabeth Swados appeared to me at that time to write bad musical plays and to be a bad writer. How much of your life can you go on being jealous? I guess you never stop. Or some people never stop. And when you hear someone talking about someone else who does the same thing you do but is more successful at it than you are, you want to squelch that other person.

My boyfriend and I slept in one of those little cubbyholes where generations of Boy Scouts had been squished. The place was full of stuff because whoever Lou had bought it from had sold it to him with all the things in it, and though they had sent truckload after truckload to junk and vintage stores, there were still shelves displaying sets of chinaware with Mexican and western motifs and antler lamps and whatever else his wife had decided to keep.

In the morning, when we got up, Lou took us around on some of his new toys, a couple of all-terrain or four-wheel-drive vehicles, things that at that time had just been developed. While they were not rich, it was definitely a lot of money to me. And there was a big crew of workers there, and the whole time we sat out by one of the ponds, this crew was mowing the lawns, coming closer and closer on tractors. I have a feeling Lou Reed did not know too much about having a staff of workers to maintain his property, or even that it might be possible to ask them to go mow farther away, and it was very apparent that these workers were going to leave the job and then go and report to others about what it was like to mow Lou Reed's lawn and fields while he was there. Even though you also kind of knew that out in Blairstown, New Jersey, at that time, about 1984, not a whole lot of locals were even going to know who Lou Reed was. Such was my vacillating perception of fame.

For a few years I did see him and Sylvia a fair bit. In the end it was my own jealousy that ended the friendship. If you don't have any shoes and nowhere to live, you don't want to admire someone's apartment and their closet contents.

on andy warhol

When he was alive, a lot of people hated Andy Warhol. He just ignored it. That is one reason I got out of the city, the way the people sneer at you. They have such contempt—until you die and suddenly they were your friend.

We used to have dinner two or three times a week, usually with Paige Powell, who was the advertising director at *Interview*.

I was never in Andy Warhol's house when he was alive. He didn't have people over. He had a big limestone house on Sixty-Sixth Street off Madison Avenue or thereabouts. I knew only one person who was in there when Andy was alive, other than his two boyfriends, who I only met after their relationships were over.

But a friend of mine, Benjamin Liu, had been to Andy's for lunch. Andy had a lot of stuff. The house was full. The kitchen was in the basement, the way it is in a lot of these old mansions in New York City. That's because when these houses were built, the people had a staff. The cook used to make the food. The cook would make the food, and the maid or butler would bring it upstairs to the family, who did not want to witness the horror of food preparation nor participate in it.

Andy did have staff, a man and a woman who I think were brother and sister from the Philippines, but they didn't live there. Anyone who has spent time talking to "staff" who work for you in your home—as housekeepers, or cooks, or whatever they do—must eventually discover or realize, these people—whether in New York or Brazil or Florida—leave their job and take all kinds of transportation to travel many hours to get home, to return to a home that (in New York City) is in one of the far reaches of another borough, the Bronx or Brooklyn or Queens, or somewhere far out. There is someone out there who, someday, will write about the modern lives of workers. Anyway, this couple, Andy's staff, weren't there that day.

Andy took Benjamin to the basement and made him Campbell's soup. That's what was on the shelves. All of the kitchen shelves were lined with Campbell's soup. I don't know what they would have cooked for him, had it not been their day off. Probably Campbell's soup.

But whether or not they were there, most of the time Andy was not.

He slept there. In the morning, the first thing he did was call Pat Hackett. He would spend an hour on the phone with her while she tape-recorded his adventures and events of the night before. He spoke to her for at least one hour a day. And when he died, she had the job to transcribe all he had said—over a period of years and years—and edit it to what she deemed the most important, for publication in his posthumous diaries.

It was her decision, what to include and what not to include. He was extremely funny and interesting and his insights and observations were brilliant. But, in addition to his thoughts and ideas and observations, he would also say (at an event, for example) "Oh! There's Barbara Eden! She looks great."

So in the morning, he would tell Pat Hackett many things, and among the things would be a comment such as, "And then we saw Barbara Eden at the Odeon—she looked great."

When Hackett edited these diaries, that was what was of interest to her: who Andy had seen and what he or she was wearing and what restaurants or clubs he had been to. Not the other stuff, his comments and remarks and ideas and thoughts. To me, his diaries are not at all what it was like to talk to him or listen to him.

Somewhere out there is the Other Diary of Andy Warhol—the pages that were not published or included—probably far more interesting.

Every day, after he talked on the phone, he went for breakfast, he went to his art factory, he had meetings, he went to lunch, he went to more meetings (with, say, advertisers or socialites). He went to a gym. He went to a dermatologist, a doctor, etc.

He went to perfume launches (I hadn't known previously that perfume companies will launch a new perfume, like a book, every season or two) or openings, readings, fashion shows.

He went to dinner, he went to premieres of movies or dance companies, he went to hear music, he went to clubs.

He went and went until he went home, about midnight or 1 A.M., and then he talked to Paige on the phone.

Then he went to sleep.

He was alone. He was lonely. He missed his mother, who he had lived with up until her death. He went to church several times a week. But when you keep that busy, you don't have to pay attention to how alone you really are.

After his death I did go into his home, and even though massive quantities of possessions had already been discarded, there was still so much stuff you could hardly get around.

If he went out, people gave him things. If he went to a perfume launch, he would get bags containing bottles. He did like perfume though, especially "Beautiful" by Estée Lauder. How many new perfumes can you have? How much perfume can you wear?

Andy grew up very poor. When you are very poor growing up, you want things.

Then, later in life, even though you don't really want stuff anymore, you can't believe it when you actually get things.

I went with Andy to the flea markets a few times. He went every weekend, and whatever he saw that he liked, he bought. I didn't have money, so for me, it was no fun. There he was, buying cookie jars and salt and pepper shakers in the shape of puffins and cowboy boots and pigs—but all I could do was just stand and watch and covet. The dealers hovered around him because they knew whatever Andy inquired about, he wasn't going to be able to bargain.

He was Andy Warhol; he was going to pay top flea-market dollar for those salt and pepper shakers that looked like pooping donkeys.

You want to have rich friends, if you are poor, but you want to have their money. But the rich people don't really want to have to spend their money on you. The richer the person, the cheaper they are.

In some ways Andy was very generous; he always took me out to dinner. On the other hand, usually the dinners were free because he had traded ad space in his magazine, *Interview*, in return for, say, seventy-five thousand dollars' worth of free dinners.

You still had to pay the tip, though, which he or Paige did. Andy was generous, in his own way. If you went to a flea market with him, he was not saying, "Gee, would you like me to buy that salt and pepper shaker you are coveting?" But he paid for dinners, or at least the tip.

And he gave me a little silk screen on canvas, at Christmas, and he and Paige bought me a winter coat one year when they couldn't stand seeing me shivering anymore, and he bought me other things, like a little beaded pocketbook. Right before he died, he told me he had a Christmas present for me, waiting at his house. But first he had to go to Milan, to show his Last Supper paintings. He didn't have a gallery in New York City. He had only had one museum retrospective, and that was eons ago. Now the only place he could show this latest work was in Italy, and it did not get good reviews. He never appeared embittered. He was kind and generous. Later, after his death, movies and biopictures came out. There was a movie about Edie Sedgwick. In the film, the character playing Edie was complaining Andy only gave her twenty-five dollars to appear in one of his movies.

Those movies—when he was alive—didn't make money; they were art. Edie was a troubled rich girl who ran through her trust fund, made an art film, and then complained she hadn't gotten paid enough.

You don't and can't expect your friends to buy things for you. That's not what I am saying.

It's just hard to know someone who is rich when you are poor.

There used to be an editor I knew at *Interview*. I would go out to dinner with that person knowing I could only get one glass of wine and an appetizer because that's all I could afford. And the editor got, like, three glasses of wine and an appetizer and a main course and dessert and when the bill came she said, "Let's split the bill."

The whole dinner, I had been counting my pennies. I ate as little as I could because I could not afford anything else.

Because I was a poor person, wanting to maintain a relationship with the editor, I was forced into this, even though she had an inheritance, a lawyer husband also with inherited money, a good-paying magazine job, an expense account, a brownstone in Brooklyn with Warhol silk screens of Mick Jagger on the wall, and a huge farmhouse in Northport, Long Island (which at that time was not the best place to have a country weekend home but was still more than I would have ever dreamed of). Yet she was not going to pay her share of dinner, let alone pay for mine.

If you have more money, you should pay if the other person is so very poor, is all I'm saying.

Andy was generous. Not mad-crazy generous, but generous. Yet the people who were his peers in the city acted scornful of this man who they said was a used-up, cheap, tight, has-been pop artist. The rage directed toward him was palpable.

One time Andy was giving a reading from his book *America* at Rizzoli Bookstore in SoHo. Some kid ran in, ripped off his wig, and ran out.

It was awful. You go to see a person—for free—and you go to hear a reading and you try to humiliate that person?

Andy was great, though. He just pulled up the hood of his leather jacket and went on reading.

Another time, a few of us were at an event at the Limelight, which was an old church that had been converted into a nightclub, and it was crowded and we were walking up the stairs and Andy was in the middle and suddenly as a group we realized: Andy was about to be attacked. We felt waves of hostility coming toward him and we knew the crowd was about to shove and push and knock him down the stairs. Involuntarily, unthinkingly, we all packed up around him and got him up the stairs in a protected fashion, into the back VIP room where there was more security. Those waves of hate and violence coming at him were scary.

He acted oblivious to it, though. If it were me, I would go home and I would cry and I would never go out again.

I don't know if it was because he was Catholic and he had to pretend everything was okay and not complain, or if he was pleased to get attention. I never did know. You could sit next to him at a movie—a bad movie—or a dance performance and you could look over and find he was fast asleep. Then afterward, "Oh, gee, that was great, wasn't it!" he said.

Many times it wasn't. But he said, "Oh, gee, that's great!" about everything.

On the one hand, acting happy and positive and upbeat is good. On the other, he had at least as many enemies for being nice as other people did who were nasty, mean, vitriolic, and gossiping.

He wanted to appear like an onion, many layers but all exactly the same; you can peel an onion and you never get down to anything different. There is no substratum.

But you could tell that he was more complicated than that. Inside there was a suffering, lonely entity.

Conversely, I have met people who wanted to appear complex and multilayered but who really were like an onion. As layer after layer fell away, there was no difference, no matter how intimate we became: their surface was the same as their depths.

i buy an apartment

In 1987 I had money for the first time, so I bought an apartment. I had saved and saved and finally had forty grand, enough to pay the deposit on an apartment under two hundred thousand.

It was a one-bedroom basement apartment, dark and over-priced, but it had a large garden. I was determined to have a garden, not a terrace. I wanted to be able to open the door for the dogs and I wanted to plant things. Note to reader: if you want to do that you should not live in New York City.

I had enough money—barely—to buy the place, from the success I had had. My success was not from *Slaves of New York* (book advance: thirty-five hundred dollars) and not from Andy Warhol's acquiring of the movie rights (purchase price: five thousand dollars). At the time when Andy said he wanted to make *Slaves of New York* into a movie, he said I could have five thousand dollars or choose one of his paintings.

"But Andy," I said, "what I really need is a place to live! I don't have anywhere to live and I can't find an apartment. You have a lot of different property in New York City, can't you let me stay in one?"

But he said no.

"Okay, I will take the five thousand dollars," I said. Because what was I going to do, with nowhere to live, walk around the streets of New York carrying a Warhol under my arm?

But I had saved money in a myriad of ways: the stories I sold to *The New Yorker*, two grants from the National Endowment for the Arts, becoming the Alfred Hodder Fellow in the Humanities at Princeton (a paid salary position), and so on, but mostly by virtue of never buying anything and never spending anything. (And some money Merchant Ivory paid for the movie rights after Andy died. Who knows how much they had to pay Andy's estate for the rights he had previously bought from me?) So finally I was able to buy an apartment and I threw all my stuff in there, still in boxes, half unpacked, and then left for my book tour.

First I went home to see my mother. "I wish there was a way I could make copies of these phonograph records," I said. "If only there was some way I could get them on tape." You see, back then we had records, and tapes. Cassette tapes. I had a tape player but no record player. My mother had a record player but no speakers. I wanted my childhood music—Marais and Miranda, for one, South African folk singers who sang, "the baboon climbed the hill." But there was no way to get the tunes heard, or to move them from one format to another.

You go to different places on a tour: the first time it's fun, the second time it's not so much fun, and by the third time, forget it. This was only my second time out, though, so I was still enjoying myself. It was for my third book, *A Cannibal in Manhattan*. (There hadn't been any budget for a tour for *American Dad*.)

This trip went west to Denver, where I stayed in a hotel with ducks that paraded through the lobby every morning, either leaving or arriving at the fountain. And it was at a reading in Denver where I randomly began complaining to the audience about my first-grade teacher, who then happened to walk through the door. It was at a bookstore in the Haight district of San Francisco where the booksellers asked me to sign a copy for Robin Williams, who had prepaid but wasn't able to make the event. But it was in L.A. when my publicist came up to me in the lobby as I was leaving. "Look, I don't know how to say this without getting you all upset, but I got a call from your neighbor," she said.

"My neighbor? Who is that?" I don't know if I had even met my new neighbors—I hadn't even stayed in my new apartment yet. "How did he get ahold of you?"

"He tracked me down through the publishing company. He was trying to find you. There's been a break-in. A robbery in your apartment."

"Oh no! What happened?"

"I'm sorry. According to your neighbor Jerry Mack, the police say your place is trashed. It's bad. They found some of your stuff in the alley, and they put it back inside."

It was midnight by the time I got home to New York. I couldn't get in; the lock had been broken. I went to my new neighbor, who lived in the matching basement apartment next to mine, and waited for the locksmith. "Yup," said Jerry. "It happened last night. I heard them. They ran. I found the stuff they dumped as they were running."

"Please, once the locksmith has the door fixed, come inside with me. I'm scared."

We went in.

It was exactly as I had left it—half-unpacked, with the boxes of clothes and other things—but nothing was missing or moved, except half a carton of orange juice from the fridge, now on the counter.

I guess the burglars were thirsty. "That's the stuff I found in the alley," Jerry said, pointing to a pile. "All your music."

It was a bunch of cassettes. They weren't mine. They must have been in the burglar's bag from a different robbery. "Look!" I said, reading the handwritten labels. "It's Marais and Miranda, the folk-singers from South Africa!"

The tapes had all the songs I wanted.

a city of rich and poor

The eighties and early nineties were years of a lot of extravagance. Because there wasn't any real Internet yet, the magazines were very important. At that time, as well, the homeless situation in the city was bad. The streets, the subways, any doorway: someone was there, defecating, pushing a shopping cart full of rotting produce, opening the door to the bank for you and demanding money for the service. The mentally ill had been given antipsychotics and released from the asylums; they dumped or exchanged their pills for stuffed animals and small gray bananas. Nothing was renovated. It was not a rich white person's city. It was not the city it is today. It was falling apart. It was a city of the homeless. And the homeless were at home.

If you went in Grand Central Terminal, it was encrusted with a patina of eighty years of smoke, soot, grime; if you went in the toilets, if you tried to sit in the waiting room, you'd be hanging out with homeless people, because that's where they lived.

A magazine editor held a big Christmas party there. She invited the hip and rich and beautiful to come to Grand Central Terminal for a dinner, followed by a performance by a young, hip choreog-

rapher and dancer at the recently renovated Brooklyn Academy of
Music. Nobody in those days went to Brooklyn; you couldn't get
there, but that was the excitement of it. That day it was bad. It
snowed and rained and flooded. But we managed to get there.

The waiting room had been cleared out. The waiting room was
clean.

For the first time in decades it didn't stink of urine. There were
no homeless people passed out on benches surrounded by piles
of bags and things stuffed in stolen shopping carts. A glittering
Christmas tree rose to the ceiling. Scented candles flickered on
ornate candelabras. Fine linens covered long tables heaped with
spiced nuts, bonbons, and baskets of flowers "by" Robert Isabell, a
famous event planner of the 1980s who commanded hundreds of
thousands of dollars for such a presentation.

The drenched and soaked guests entered this room: at any entrance, heavy red velvet ropes had been erected to block the regular
commuters at Grand Central Terminal from coming in.

But most commuters didn't even use this waiting room. The
people who used this waiting room—where they slept, where they
lived—were the homeless. Tonight they were prevented from re-
turning.

So, as the New York City Gay Men's Chorus sang, the homeless, in great stinking crowds, gathered at the ropes, pressing up in
filthy rags, to look in at the attendees.

The homeless could be prevented from using the waiting room
that one night.

But they could not be blocked from the restrooms. You went in
that women's room in your evening gown, and—taking a bath
in the sink next to yours, or passed out in a toilet stall—that's
where they were.

I don't know if any of them even got a piece of cake.

Maybe a half million was spent there that night, maybe more.

It was a scene worthy of Dickens, but somehow nothing other than the glitz and glamour ever got written up by the press. A day or two later, it's all forgotten: just another party in New York City. And I still haven't figured out a novel to put that scene into.

how i met the kennedys

It was about 1961 or 1962 when John F. Kennedy gave a speech at Amherst College and people gathered to greet him as he walked through the campus. My father took me to see this man. He held me up in his arms, and as Kennedy came through he stopped and shook my hand and said hello. I remember this vividly because even at that age this man made a strong impression on me. I felt he liked me, that he had singled me out for special attention and there was even something—not sexual, but the man had a sexual charisma that even a tiny girl was aware of.

Years passed and I was made over by a beauty magazine to look like a rich person. That same evening a friend took me to the opening night of the ballet season and whisked me into the VIP or board members room. I was wearing a borrowed Oscar de la Renta suit, and Jackie Kennedy Onassis came up to me. She looked at me with a mix of amusement, curiosity, and bafflement. Then she took a tiny pair of spectacles from her handbag and put them on. She looked me up and down and shook hands with me. I did not know it or realize it at the time, but not only had I been perfectly groomed by the magazine staff to successfully resemble a rich socialite, which took ten hours, but I was also wearing the line from de la Renta that was not supposed to be ready for months and that no one was supposed to have access to yet. It was a big deal. Boaz, de la Renta's assistant, rushed over and started shouting at me, "Where did you get that suit! How did you get it!"

The magazine had dressed me in that suit and told me to go out in it for the night and have fun; it was part of the story I was writing. I did not know I was not meant to be wearing that suit. I did not know who Boaz was. "None of your business!" I said, giggling, although I put it much more politely, and I went back to chatting with Jackie O.

Another night, at a different friend's house, at a small dinner, I was seated next to Caroline Kennedy Schlossberg. She was very nice but you could see she could never make any new friends—she had only those she had grown up with—and I understood this perfectly. Who would she ever be able to trust? I was a writer, and besides, that evening I was not dressed to resemble a wealthy socialite.

Then, after another event, there was a small reception and John F. Kennedy Jr. was there, and my friend introduced us. He was good looking but a lot younger than me, and I felt way out of my league. Besides, I was very plain.

He, too, had an animal magnetism but not as interesting; it was the sexuality of the frat boy, not my thing. Of this famous family, three of the four are dead. (It seems curious to me that I met all of them, at different times and places and stages in my life, but also pointless.) It makes me think of Forrest Gump. But in my case, I'm spliced into photographs that exist only in my head. At a certain point, you get old, you realize, Hey! I met all these original Kennedys! And then you think, but what does it mean? Why? Finally I thought of an answer: I don't know.

socialites, art, and fashion

For a long time my life in New York was interesting to me. If, over a period of time, I would meet various socialites, I would think, Now I am meeting various socialites. And I would try to discern something about that breed.

I met Lee Radziwill once—not that she counts as one of the main or original John F. Kennedy family, but still. The most interesting thing about her was that she was so thin. She appeared to be a woman who had spent her entire life not eating, or consuming only enough calories to sustain life. I could not imagine this, a whole lifetime devoted to not eating. She had the look of doelike suffering and yet superiority, not just because of her social status, but because of her vast suffering. I am sure she suffered a great deal, but by the time you get to a certain age, you kind of realize everyone has suffered a great deal. You are not unique.

When you met Nancy Reagan in person you saw that she, too, had spent a lifetime not eating. The photos do add on pounds. Starved magazine editors, there are quite a number of those. I don't know how they do it because they go out to eat all the time, breakfast and lunch and dinner, and even if they go to the gym, most of their day is pretty inactive, and when you get older and your metabolism slows, the weight doesn't just come off easily once you have put it on.

And all of those women will probably tell you, "Oh, I eat." But they can't be eating. They have the big heads and the toothpick limbs that could snap at any moment. Further, it is not fun. No matter what you look like, when you spend time with one of these women you not only feel fat but expect to be responsible for one of their twigs snapping off.

New York City trends change. When I first moved back to the city after college in the 1980s, you could somehow afford an apartment. SoHo was still a working neighborhood; inside the cast-iron buildings there were factories making buttons or pins; artists were living there illegally; and on the ground-floor levels small art galleries opened up—there were all these kids making art and dealers were showing it, and just by accident I found out you could head there on a Saturday night and there were openings happening, people spilling out from the galleries onto the otherwise deserted streets.

Back then, even if you couldn't afford a painting or an artwork, you still got to mingle and it was a party. And there were peculiar nightclubs, and the people at the art opening would say, "Are you going to—" and name a place, Danceteria, the Mudd Club, Save the Robots, Beulah Land, Area, the Pyramid Club, whatever was going on at the time, with performances and music. It was all just a big scene. I always thought it too bad that I had missed the 1960s in New York.

I didn't realize how unique or special the times were that I was living in now, the eighties.

You could be broke but still have an amazing life. People were still able to find really cheap apartments, not that you would necessarily want to live in them. An old hotel had been converted into apartments and somehow a guy I knew was able to rent the coat checkroom. It had a great address downtown, but of course a coat checkroom is small, it doesn't have windows, and I think there was a toilet but no shower. That was his home.

Even so, I don't know how anybody ever made money to pay rent. A place might cost five or six hundred dollars, but a lot of people displayed no visible signs of employment. Did everyone but me have a family who sent them money?

I had a job writing for a downtown newspaper. I wrote funny little articles, reviewing art shows or clubs or events. I got paid twenty bucks an article, not enough to survive on—and then they fired me! The next week I was on the cover of *New York* magazine. That was an odd transformation. My book *Slaves of New York* wasn't in any stores because the publisher hadn't printed many copies. I was broke and paranoid, except now when I went someplace and people started whispering, I wasn't being paranoid. They were actually whispering.

Then the trend—art being something cutting edge—changed. The gallery spaces cost so much for the dealers to rent, they had to sell art for a lot of money and they only wanted rich people in their galleries.

After that, for a while, fashion shows became the social event.

Going to a fashion show is fun the first few times. Then you realize: I can't afford the clothes even if I do think they are pretty. And most of them are only pretty because they are being worn by a beautiful six-foot-tall twenty-year-old girl. If I wore a pair of baggy silk shorts and a blouse with one long sleeve and one bare shoulder with a large lumpy knot in the back just at the base of the spine in turquoise with beige spots, it would not look good. And if I wore six-inch platform shoes I would fall over.

The clothes cost thousands and thousands of dollars and the main objective is for people to say they attended the show. The people who go to the shows in New York City are all dressed quite boringly, usually in black, and would never wear the things that are being worn by the models onstage.

So the people watching isn't all that fun, either. The front row might have some familiar faces of magazine editors or one or two celebrities or a department store buyer. There might be a "writer" who once wrote a tiny book of "funny" essays thirty years ago that no one has ever read but is so short people think they read it and remember it was funny. There are people who are "important" and other people take their pictures with cell phones or try to stop them for a mini-interview for some fashion channel. The other people are like, "So-and-so was there, and so-and-so."

The other rows are filled with junior editors and PR people. They are sitting there talking on their cell phones, texting and tweeting, to say who is there and that they are at such and such a show—but the whole time there is a general rage that they are not seated in the important first row. Then you wait and you wait and you wait and then there is very loud music and some girls or boys come out wearing these different outfits. Then it is over.

You just sit there and you think, Ooo, pretty.

Even if I could buy it, I would get a stain on it or it would make me look dumpy or whatever. You might as well be one of a school of fish or a bunch of sparrows. I don't really like the job of sitting there as an unpaid interested audience member. I mean, I will be an audience member, but pay me. Or give me a dress.

my mom gets a job and a real home

Eventually my mom got a job. Because she wrote poetry, A. R. Ammons selected her to come to Cornell University. She was fifty years old.

My mother lived on a small private road just off the college campus. It was a historic district. You couldn't touch or change anything on the house unless it was done according to historic code. This made it hard to keep her house warm. Her house had windows with crisscross wood that formed diamond panes, very old and good at keeping in the cold.

The place was basically air-conditioned in summer, only there was no air-conditioning. In winter, it was so air-conditioned I had to stop visiting her, after I took out my contact lenses and put them in their case and left them on the windowsill overnight. In the morning, when I got up, the contact lenses had frozen into two little chunks of ice.

There were a few other charming houses on my mom's street in Ithaca. One had been a chicken coop, another had been a barn. Everyone knew each other on this little block, and because it was a private road, the neighborhood had to gang up together to pay for private snowplowing or to get the garbage collected.

There were a lot of rules about garbage. Garbage night was a big night. The garbage company came at around 4 A.M. to get the garbage. You had to prepare the garbage carefully or you got in trouble. Days before the event, my mother began talking about it. "We have to get the garbage ready. It has to be perfect."

Initially I thought she was overreacting. The next day I went out to check. This was slapped on the bin:

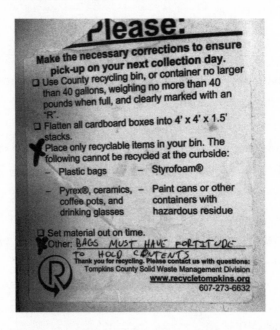

If you made a mistake you got this Day-Glo warning stuck on the garbage, which was now strewn around in front—to teach you a lesson. You knew you were in a university town because the garbage collector took the time to write BAGS MUST HAVE FORTITUDE. He probably had a degree. I wouldn't be able to be a garbage collector in that town. If I were collecting garbage at 3 or 4 A.M. and there was this terrible violation, I would write BAG BROKE.

There were even bigger enforcement threats this garbage company could level on you. If your garbage was incorrect—in any way—and they were feeling generous, you were issued just the warning, but after that, you got a ticket. A garbage ticket carried serious penalties with it. And so, Monday morning, it was always with some trepidation that you went out to check whether the garbage had been accepted and carried away. Or you would find a warning, a ticket, or the garbage flung back at the house.

My mom lived on that block for thirty years. Once, there had been a big mansion, but it had been torn down to make apartments. The houses that were left on that block had been part of the original estate. My mom, for example, was living in the "gatekeeper's cottage." For a lot of years, a family we called the Beautiful Family lived next door to her in the "gardener's cottage." They were all beautiful, those Nolan-Wheatleys. There was the handsome English husband who had grown up in Singapore and taught Chinese, the beautiful mother from New Orleans who had grown up in a vampire-style mansion, which was later used as a set in films.

In any southern Gothic horror movie set in New Orleans, to this day, you can see that house. The Beautiful Family didn't personally own it—it belonged to the larger consortium of the Beautiful Family's mother. Her big southern family had grown up there, all of them inheriting a fraction or portion of the spoils, and they now all reaped the benefits of having had to live in a place crawling with cockroaches and the ghosts of slaves.

And then there were their four beautiful daughters. They all took ballet, although one might have played the piano—not sure. These four daughters had long hair; you know what I'm talking about? Tresses? Dark, flowing tresses?

The Beautiful Family would have us over and serve real lemonade in a glass pitcher, sometimes in the yard, made out of fresh-squeezed lemons. The yard was small and lovely, full of fragrant flowers, that kind of thing, and when this beautiful family sat out there, the handsome father with his English accent, chatting away in Chinese to himself, and the mother with her lovely New Orleans drawl, not imbibing any alcoholic beverages, and those four daughters just twirling away, on pointe, with their hair flowing, you felt privileged to know them.

Everyone on the block used to know each other and they had parties and get-togethers. It was very sad when the Beautiful Family left, and Bernice (she lived in the "old barn") went to a nursing home and then died, and Tony (the "chicken coop") moved, etc. But my mom was so happy to be living in such a nice house, on this pleasant street, and to be a professor at Cornell.

After the Beautiful Family left there were a few other residents next door. Then, some time later, a new couple moved in. In the yard I met the new neighbor.

"Hi," he said over the fence.

"Oh, hi," I said. "It's nice to meet you."

"I have a daughter. She's my *biological* daughter. I used to live next door to her mother and her girlfriend. They were trying to get pregnant but they couldn't. They kept saying, 'If this takes any longer, we're going to go and blow up a sperm bank!' 'I'm here for you,' I told them. The three of us had only one kid before they got their operations. Then they got married and her parents disowned them. My daughter doesn't live with me but she comes here to visit. Is Willow your only child? Did you ever think of having more?"

"Oh, I'm okay," I said.

It was, for me, maybe kind of too much information. But still the neighbors seemed nice enough.

He was busy redoing the garden of fragrant flowers where the Beautiful Family had formerly entertained by serving nonalcoholic beverages. Pretty soon he had blocked off the street with a few tons of stone and was busy paving over the backyard and putting up a large shed, right by the property line.

Eventually, he planned to use this shed as a small private museum for his wife's collection of salt and pepper shakers. She had more than two thousand salt and pepper shakers and nowhere to display them, until he built her this storage shed on the property line, which, along with a lot of building materials, wheelbarrows, and piles of cement that they kept there, created a very sturdy barricade and arresting visual.

You know, you have neighbors. In the country, they do things like that, slapping up a building right on the property line without a permit, and what are you going to do? You keep your mouth shut and try to get along.

They were good people. When I went out to garden, it was hard work. It was hot. I had to pull up weeds. Then the neighbor appeared. He tried to help. He shouted, "You look stressed! You should take up meditation."

I did not want to get angry with the neighbor. I did not want to explain to him, if you are gardening you don't need to take up meditation, it *is* a form of meditation.

As soon as I tried to get some kind of yard work done, he would appear to remind me to meditate. I had been perfectly calm and peaceful until I got the meditation command, but you can't start shouting back, "I don't NEED to meditate! I don't WANT to meditate! I WON'T meditate!"

When I had calmed down a bit he came and leaned over the fence. "Feeling any calmer now?"

That was what it was, I guess, to have a neighbor up there. You are more careful about your privacy when you live in a city apartment. You don't get involved with your apartment neighbors if you can help it. In the city, only a wall separates you. Here, there was a little yard.

I saw him on the street by the house, when I had taken the bus up from the city. He was walking his dog, and when he saw me he opened his arms in a wide embrace.

I hugged him back. "Hi!"

"Ooo, what's going on here?" he mumbled in my ear and pressed up against me. "That's quite a greeting." How could I hug him in a friendly response ever again? Maybe he would say he got definite "vibes" from me. But there were no vibes! To me, if a man has a ponytail but is bald on top, I am not giving him any vibes. I don't like ponytails, not on men; that's my own problem.

I was sitting in a hanging chair that was on the side porch. The neighbor was walking with his wife and dog. "You look like you are sitting in a sex chair!" he shouted.

I winced. What was a sex chair, anyway? Now I could never sit in that hanging chair again.

ithaca is the wrong place

I'm just trying to explain why I thought it was better for me to sell my mom's house, after I couldn't look after her at home, and go somewhere without people nearby. I just could not keep out of trouble, I could not keep doing bad things. I was on the bus again in the middle of the day, headed back from the city, when I got a call from the police. "We got a call from your neighbors, saying your dogs are barking."

"Oh my gosh. I'm so sorry. I am on the bus coming home. I just spoke to my child; she was at home twenty minutes ago. She said she was going out for a little bit and she must have forgotten to shut the back door."

I called up the neighbor right away and apologized. I felt so bad. It was the second time that back door had been left open when no one was home and the dogs had gone out and barked. I had told him at the time, "Please, if that ever happens again, just go around to my mom's house and shoo the dogs inside and shut the door."

I didn't have parties, I didn't play music late at night, but once in a while—this was the second time—those dogs did bark, and so it was no wonder the neighbor went to the police. Although, come to think of it, his did, too.

Then someone began to vandalize the property. I had a big rhododendron bush in the front that I had planted there for my mom, twenty years earlier. Day after day someone walked along and broke off branches.

Some kid? I don't know. Just wrecking this lovely shrub. They broke off all the tips that were going to bloom, they broke off the branches . . . Was this shrub impinging on someone's walk? Yes. A few limbs stuck out. I figured, this was a private street—any pedestrian was free to walk there, and, on their walk, could easily walk around it by taking a step onto the street and back onto the sidewalk. Or, if the shrub bothered you, you could leave a note on the front door of the house where that shrub is planted. "Hi! I like to walk here and your shrub has been bothering me. Would you mind pruning?"

I mean, the home health worker had no qualms leaving a note on the front door complaining about my mom's hygiene and physical state. I don't think anyone would be too shy, in that area, to complain about a shrub with protruding limbs. But, whatever. I was guessing there was some kind of criminal in the area, possibly a student, who enjoyed hurting plants.

Come spring, after it bloomed, I would prune that tree at the appropriate time. Meanwhile, though, I placed an expensive traffic cone (seventeen dollars from a hardware store) in front of that shrub as a protective barricade.

The shrub molester took the cone and broke off more branches.

They took that cone and they threw it into someone else's yard, a few blocks away. But I did not find the cone right away. It was gone, and my shrub was further attacked. So I bought another cone (seventeen dollars) and a "caution" sign (seventeen dollars) to put in front of that shrub, and I put a stake in the ground to tie that sign—and stake the cone—onto the sidewalk.

This picture does not show the full construction I built to protect that shrub, I just have it here to give you an idea. But the shrub hater broke off more branches of my rhododendron that was about to burst into bloom once the winter chill had passed in another eight to ten months, maybe a bit longer depending on whether or not this was a good year or bad, and that shrub hater took my sign and my ropes and my stakes and my cone and threw them somewhere, littering the landscape.

So I bought more things to protect that shrub. I got more cones and tied the cones to some string and I wrapped the string around the shrub. And the person with the vendetta against the shrub pulled everything down and broke off more stalks.

I reapplied my shrub protection. This time I took a bag of mulch and I put it on top of the base of the cone and the stake to weigh it down so that it would not be so easy to move, since the bag of mulch (seventeen dollars at the local supply store) weighed forty pounds, and then I tied a bunch of wind chimes (very lovely, seventeen dollars in a gift shop) on the whole structure and on the shrub, so when that shrub hater came along I would hear him or her trying to break the shrub branches and stealing those things I had used to protect it.

But by the time the anti-landscaping person jingled the wind chimes and I got out there, they were gone and the further damage was done. So I rebuilt. And then I poured a few things on the branches to discourage the person who hated my shrub, so that my shrub would teach whoever was trying to hurt it a lesson, and that the person's gloves would remember not to do that again. I spritzed deer repellent (seventeen dollars) made out of coyote and fox urine and rotten eggs, that was alleged to keep the deer from eating your garden plants, guaranteed to provide six months of foul odor, and I added some maple syrup (seventeen dollars, but I didn't use the whole bottle) to make sure the deer repellent stuck. And I added some hot sauce. After all, I thought, probably I was being paranoid and it was just one of the local deer at work.

If it was a deer, the maple syrup might attract the deer to the shrub where it would taste the hot sauce and simultaneously be repelled by the deer repellent causing it to bolt into the ropes and stakes and set off the wind chimes, which would make so much noise I would be able to hear the noise, run to the antique historic diamond pane crisscross windows and look out there and SEE what was at that shrub doing the damage.

But if it was a student, walking by on their way to the campus and hurting my twenty-year-old rhododendron just for fun on their way to class, it was my belief that when he or she went to class no one would want to sit next to them, smelling like fox urine and rotten eggs, smearing hot sauce on their desk. And handing in papers sticky with maple syrup would not result in a good grade.

From now on, any person or deer who wanted to try to steal the cones on the sidewalk and the sign suggesting the person walk around rather than wound the shrub, he or she or the deer would learn a lesson, or their nice winter gloves would be spoiled.

But it was only a short time after I set up this system when the neighbor called me. "Tama! You can't have a bag of mulch on the sidewalk!"

No preliminary "Hi, is this a bad time?" No "Listen, I have some concerns . . ."

No, he just launched into yelling.

Then he had a lawyer send me a threatening letter saying he was going to sue me.

life in the old days

Before I moved into my mom's house I would take the bus up from Brooklyn every few weeks to check on her. She was falling a lot during this time. Mom was not always so easily reachable, and because she did not always know how to hang up the phone, it would remain busy for days. I wouldn't be able to reach Mom, nor could the neighbor, and after a couple of days, when my mom didn't respond, the neighbor (who had her key) went over and found she had fallen again.

Where I grew up, after the divorce, we had a party line. A party line means everybody on that same stretch of road had the same telephone line. If the phone call was for your house, you knew your ring—it might be one short ring and two long rings. Your neighbor might have the ring long, short, long. Anybody who got a phone call, all the phones on the party line would ring, but you knew not to answer it unless it was your home's ring. If you picked up the phone and you wanted to make a call, but your neighbor had already made a call, you would hear your neighbor on the phone and hang up and hope they did not blab for a long time so you could use the line to call. Sometimes, if you were on a call, if they wanted, the neighbor might listen in, which was just not considered decent. But people did it.

I am not sure how this could be in my lifetime, unless I am a *lot* older than I am admitting. Still, I would know, right? These telephones, they were rotary phones. They had a dial with numbers on it. When you dialed, you put your finger in the hole and turned this whole wheel, which would slowly revolve back to the original position. Touch-tone came later, with buttons instead of a dial. If you wanted to make a transatlantic call—not that anybody in the area knew a foreign person—you had to get the operator to "place the call." They might tell you to hang up and call you back after they had procured a transatlantic line, because sometimes those transatlantic lines were busy.

The phone was attached to the wall by a cord, and not a cord with a jack you could unplug. It was permanently tied to the wall, so you had a "telephone table" and a chair placed there so you could sit and speak, since you couldn't move while you were on it. There weren't remote controls for televisions, either, but that's a different discussion.

If you were very rich, you might have more than one phone in your house, but nobody around there was rich.

Now, living with Mom, even though there was a phone in every room and no one else sharing the line, you still couldn't make a phone call. There was always a phone left somewhere that had not been hung up. Mom didn't like me using her phone, either. It had only been a year since she retired from Cornell at age eighty, but her physical deterioration was profound.

SHORTLY AFTER I MOVED IN, my mother fell and hit her head. I called the ambulance and went separately to the hospital. She had been strapped to a board. "I have to use the toilet," she said to me.

"My mom needs the toilet," I told the nurse.

"No," the nurse snarled. "She can't. She's tied up!"

"Please help her," I said. "The home health aide had just arrived to bathe her when she fell. She needs to be washed."

"No," the nurse said.

Hours passed. "My mom wants something to drink, she's very thirsty."

"No."

More time passed. "My mom is hungry. My mom has been tied up here for five hours. Please, can't you do something?"

"No. She hit her head. She must remain strapped down."

The nurse went to join the others at a party out by the station. After six hours a nurse practitioner came in and untied my mom. "Her head is cut," the woman said. "Where's my staple gun?"

It would take five minutes to gently sew the cut on her head, but the stapler speeded things up.

After that a doctor arrived. "Okay," he said. "You can take her home."

"I can't!" I said. "She's dehydrated and hasn't eaten all day. She's incoherent. And she can't even sit up."

"She's fine," the doctor said. "Get her out of here."

"I'm telling you, she's not able to move. How am I going to get her in the car?"

"Nothing wrong with her." Finally he looked at her directly. "How many children do you have?"

"I don't," my mother said weakly.

"How many children does your mother have?" the doctor said.

"Two," I said.

He turned to my mother again. "Okay, who is this?" He pointed at me.

"I don't know," my mother said.

"She's fine!" the doctor said. "She's able to answer. This wasn't an emergency, I can't admit her. You should have taken her to a doctor. Anybody could have sewed up her head."

"But . . . it's Labor Day. Her doctor's office is closed. Even if she is wheeled out to the car and someone helps me get her in, I don't think I can get her out when we get home, let alone in the house."

"I'm not going to approve any decision to keep her overnight. She can stay here, but you are going to be charged thousands to have her stay overnight."

There was nothing I could do; my mother was too weak and dehydrated to move. When he saw I wasn't going to take her, he decided that he would sign her in as needing a CAT scan or something so that she would be admitted.

A day or so later the home health service I had hired daily staff from called. "We aren't supposed to tell you this," they said, "but we wanted to give you a heads-up: someone at the hospital called Adult Protective Services and turned you in."

"What?" I said.

"We got a call from Adult Protective Services saying your mother was admitted to the hospital. She was dirty, hungry, and dehydrated."

"But . . ."

A day or so later there was a knock on the door. "Hello?"

"I'm here from Adult Protective Services. I've come to see your mother and talk to you. I'm not allowed to tell you who reported you."

She sat with me and my mom for a long time. I told her I had help on a daily basis and that I had already contacted a nursing home, nearby, even before my mom's fall. I told her the hospital knew all this, and that I had taken her there after she fell.

"I don't know why the hospital turned you in," she said.

Now I couldn't sleep. Was living here any different than Communist Russia, where your neighbor could call up the KGB to come and get you and take you to the Gulag? What if someone— maybe my neighbor!—called Child Protective Services? The next visit might be from a different social worker, trying to take my kid away!

I REALIZED I NEEDED HELP. I saw an advertisement for a psychiatrist and gave him a call. I went to his office, which was attached to his house on the lake and smelled like pot. Dr. Sandor F— told me his life story, how he was not Jewish.

He had been a neurosurgeon but then became a psychiatrist and had worked for Adult Protective Services—or a similar government department—before going into private practice. "Once they've come to your house and were unable to find anything wrong, they can't keep coming back," he said about APS.

Then he told me a long story about Eckhart Tolle. "He was a very ugly man who was a failure," he said. "When he was in his twenties he decided to kill himself. He lay on the floor when he had a revelation: he should stop feeling bad. So he got up and wrote a bestselling book, which enabled him, although ugly and a failure, to make a lot of money and get a beautiful Japanese girlfriend."

I didn't quite follow what the doctor said.

Then he gave me a prescription for some anti-anxiety pills and told me to make a follow-up appointment.

The follow-up appointment was going to cost less than the initial visit of $250, but I still didn't have another $150 to get the rest of his life story, so I just started taking the pills.

Even though he said Adult Protective Services wasn't going to come back, I was still upset. All I had been doing, day in and day out, was trying to look after my kid and my mom. What kind of hospital would tie an eighty-year-old woman to the bed for six hours and then turn in the person who had brought her for help? So I wrote a letter to the hospital.

There was no answer. I wrote again. I saw an ad in the paper; all the people who were on the fundraising board of this hospital were going to hold a grand benefit gala. I sent my letter to all those people on the benefit committee. I wanted to tell them: you are fundraising for a hospital who leaves old people bound to a bed for six hours, while the nurses and doctors gather for a party at the nurse's station.

After I sent out the letter again, a man telephoned. "Are you Tama Janowitz?" he said. "I'm from hospital publicity. I looked you up on the computer. You're famous. Will you come to the hospital to discuss our writing a letter of apology to you?"

I went to see him. The man in PR was very intrigued with me. He brought in the head nurse and they both looked at me. "We're not going to write a letter of apology to you. We just wanted to see you in person."

MOM FELL MORE FREQUENTLY. I took her to every type of doctor, for every type of test. We went to a neurologist who was young and from some South American country. He hit her on her leg with a hammer. "Ow," my mom said.

"Oops," the doctor said. "Sorry, I was aiming for your knee."

He hit her again and her leg twitched. "Very good!" he said. "Now, listen to this sentence: a brown fox jumped over a sleeping dog." He looked out the door down the hall. A receptionist was leading a young cute girl, his next patient, to another room.

"A brown fox jumped over a sleeping dog," my mom said.

"Okay," he said. "Now I would like you to draw a picture of a clock, with the hands at twenty to four."

Her image was as good as one of Salvador Dalí's. She had made an oval, with a few numbers in random places on the clock face and two lines pointing down.

Mom could never draw real well anyway.

"Okay," the neurologist said to my mother. "You're fine. You can go." He turned to me. "Your mom has no signs of dementia."

"I didn't bring her to you for dementia," I said. "She's always been like this; me, too. I brought her to see you because of her legs. Her legs!" I said. "She came here because her legs hurt her, terribly! And she falls."

"I don't know," he said. "You might want to take her for some other tests."

"What about the sentence?"

He was looking anxiously out the door, down the hall, to the next patient. "What sentence?"

"The fox jumped over the dog!" I said. "You asked her to listen to it. Aren't you going to ask her to repeat it now that some time has passed?"

"Oh," he said. "No." He looked down the hall once more with eager trepidation. "That's not why I said that sentence."

Eventually I took my mom to a nursing home. It was a small place in an old house that only took six residents and where there was a lot of staff. After a week, the owner called. "You have until the end of the month to find a new place for your mom," she said.

"I'm sorry, she requires too much care, much more than we can provide here."

"Whaaa?" I said. "You said you could look after her! What did my mom do?"

"She falls. She's angry at her roommate. She might wander out. We have stairs here. She goes in other people's rooms. Don't get me wrong, we are all very fond of her."

This was all very strange to hear, but nonetheless I found another place. The new place was nearer the hospital where my mom had been left tied up in her own waste for six hours, but it was also closer to her house. I wouldn't be spending an hour each day driving to see her. It was more institutional than the old farmhouse had been, but it was still nice. She had her own room and there were other people there, in bibs and diapers, who hung out in the big room at the front where a nurse's aide would play "memory games"—questions out of a big book. I took my mom in to participate on one such instance. I sat her on the couch. Dale, another resident, came in. Dale was very agitated. "How are you, Dale?" I said. "Have a seat!"

"Oh, thank you," said Dale. She sat down heavily, seemingly on top of my mother.

"Who wrote, 'Romeo, Romeo, wherefore art thou, Romeo'?" the nurse's aide said.

No one responded. The aide turned the page for the answer. "It was Paul Revere!" she said. A general malaise flowed on the surface of the river of Alzheimer's and dementia in the room. I couldn't contain myself and I squeaked. The nonverbal discomfort escalated.

"Oh, wrong page!" the nurse's aide said at last, turning back a leaf in the book as she announced, "It was Shakespeare. *William* Shakespeare."

THE INMATES CAME AND WENT. Sometimes when you got there, everybody had been herded into the back of the dining room; someone was dead, and they were waiting for the ambulance. There was Dale, she would come into my mom's room and get in the closet. There was Joan, who followed me around, saying, as she did to everyone: "Ma'am! Ma'am! Can you help me?" But no help could be provided. The people with dementia and Alzheimer's, they are scary. They grab you, they glare, they touch you, they throw things. If they were babies, and cute, you wouldn't mind so much and it would seem normal. With the old people, no. Drooling, snot, it's excusable only in formative years. Otherwise, it is not attractive. Joan followed me into the business office. I was scared. "Ma'am! Ma'am!"

"Joan?"

"Ma'am!"

"Joan?"

"Ma'am!"

The director cut in. "Joan! That's enough now!"

"Why? You're spoiling our duet!"

There was a woman who sat silently at a table at every mealtime, not eating, tears streaming down her face. There were people who brought in service dogs, there were a couple of cats who lived there, and there were fish. There were students who came in and played the violin and the piano; there were religious groups who came in to preach. It was a vivid setting, it was overwhelming, you were involved in the daily routine and activities. There were singalongs. There was searching for my mom, who would always manage to get in someone else's room and get into his or her bed for a nap. There was the staff.

There was an aide who was affectionate with Mom, maybe too affectionate; whenever I was there, she was with my mom, playing

with her hair, stroking her, telling her, "I'm your other daughter."
She liked to hug me, too. "Where are you going?" she said.

"I have to go shopping."

"Oh, bring me something!"

I bought her a pie.

"Can we have a spa day together?" I gave her a gift certificate
for a massage at the spa. Then they moved the aide away from
patients—into the kitchen. I liked her, but it was a relief in a way to
not have to see her. She and her husband lived with his parents. I
got an e-mail from her saying she had been fired and had no money
and her unemployed husband had left her. I didn't know what to
do. These people become your family.

You can't stand being there. You have to be there, you look at
the clock, it's your mom, you take her out, you go to a restaurant,
you can't get her out of the car, you get her back to the nursing
home. You go home, you come back the next day. I walked into
the library. There was a family sitting with one of the patients, the
beautiful woman who wept at each meal. The man looked familiar.
Maybe I had seen him before. I smiled at him but he just scowled
at me. What did he think? He acted as if I were trying to get his
autograph. It wasn't a private room, it was the library of ancient
*National Geographic*s and large print *Reader's Digest*s. I left.

Then I went to my mom's room. I thought, That was John
Lithgow, the actor. My life had become very sad indeed. If I was
going to hallucinate a movie star at this nursing home, did I really have to hallucinate John Lithgow? I was alone too much. My
daughter was living with me, but she had a boyfriend and she was
busy with after-school activities, and now I had sunk so low that
I was inventing visiting movie stars at the home, but not sexy or
hot movie stars or ones that I liked, just a scowling, irritated John

Lithgow. "I'm going to move in here," I told my mom. "As soon as a room opens up."

"You can have my bed," my mom said.

It turned out it *was* John Lithgow, though. He came a couple of times a year to visit his mother, who was the weeping woman. Then she died, so I didn't have those hallucinations anymore.

My mom lasted a year this time before they told me I had to get her into somewhere with an even higher level of care. By now she couldn't walk at all. Her legs did not support her, not even to get up out of bed. Her doctor told me here as well, "But there's nothing wrong with her."

I found her a new nursing home. I did the paperwork, I got her into the car, I got her to that new place. If I had taken notes, this kind of thing would be an entire book. You don't want to remember. You don't want to dwell.

During this entire debacle, I still went into that supermarket to get her the candy she liked.

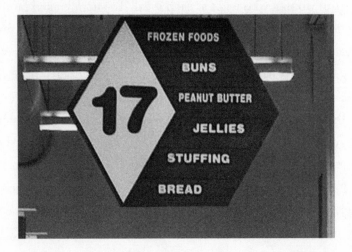

Let's recount this again. Let's say you want a bun. You would go to the aisle that says "Bread." You would not start looking for the "Bun" aisle. No. You might as well put crunchy peanut butter in a different aisle than creamy. WHY DO I KEEP GOING BACK TO THAT SUPERMARKET? I'm sick, that's why.

DAY AFTER DAY, VISITING MY MOM. It was so sad. I wanted my mom. My mom was vanishing. Parts of her mind disappeared. Then, the next day, something would be back. It was like trying to call someone internationally, someone up on Mount Everest, with a bad connection. You could hear a word, you could hear two, you got excited, you were going to speak. Then the wind got too strong.

Now, most days when I went to see her, she was further away. She was lying on her bed every time I went there, kind of contorted, and she couldn't seem to look at me. Even I was starting to realize, the holes in her brain were getting bigger. The Swiss cheese up there was melting.

"Hi Mom! How are you?"

"I am looking for my box."

"Your box?"

"I am looking for my lockbox."

"Your . . . lockbox?"

"My *lox* box. A flying lox box."

"Huh?"

"Where is my box? Where is my lox box? Where is my flying lox box?"

I could join in with her, sometimes, for a little bit. We could riff on lockboxes and lox boxes and flying lox. It was better than not connecting at all.

As different areas of the mind got eaten away there would be a brief burst as a different part took over. For a while, if you could get on that level, you could almost have a conversation. Actually, she did make sense in a certain *Alice in Wonderland* wordplay kind of way, and I knew her humor.

Sometimes, we could both just jump on the same page—like, the phone was ringing and she said, "What is that sound?"

"The telephone."

"The telephone? What's it doing?"

"It's ringing, Mom."

"Who is it?"

"How would I know who's on the other end? It's ringing."

"That's not a telephone."

"That's the telephone. It was invented by Alexander Graham Bell."

"No, he did not invent the phone."

"Yes, he did. He said, 'Watson, can you hear me?'"

"Who was Watson?"

"The guy on the other end!"

"The other end of what?"

"On the other end of the phone."

"How did he know to pick it up?"

"Good point. I don't know . . . I guess . . . it was ringing?"

"And so he picked it up and said, 'Hello'?"

"I don't know. I guess."

"How would he know what to do, unless it was ringing?"

"Right."

"So why did Bell call him?"

"I mean, there was nobody else to call! There was only one other phone!"

"If there was only one other phone, why would Bell need to call him?"

"To say hello?"

"What number was it that he called, then?"

"One. It was number one."

It could go on like this for quite some time. It was a "oneness" of nonsense. And both of us would laugh, a lot, but whether or not for the same reason I don't know.

how to inspire rage

Meanwhile, every time I got back to my mom's house from visiting her in the nursing home every day, I was scared of Adult Protective Services. Despite the psychiatrist's words, I still thought they might show up again. There was the neighbor, and the freezing cold house falling apart that I kept trying to get fixed up. My mom had been so scared of being broke that she had never had anything fixed there in thirty years. It was falling down. The police showed up when my dogs barked, even though there were plenty of other barking dogs around, including the neighbor's.

I was used to people's anger, however. There are some people on this planet who irritate others. It wasn't intentional, but I was one of them.

example one

Once there was a television producer and his wife, who was a very well-known romance writer, who had an idea for a brilliant television series and thought I should write it. The television producer called me up, right after I started publishing stories in *The New*

Yorker, and asked if I would be interested in writing the bible—and more—for this television series based on his wife's idea.

"What's a bible?"

"A bible for a TV series," he explained. I still didn't know. He sighed. "It's a book of chapters on each of the people in this TV series, who they are, where they grew up, their natures and personalities. It would contain everything you can think of regarding these characters and their lives. Your job would be to write the bible, and then come up with the episodes, the plots, the stories, the dialogue, first write the initial pilot for the series, and then write maybe twenty or thirty episodes."

He said he would pay me twenty grand if I did it.

I was very excited. Not just that I would get paid twenty thousand dollars, but that someone knew I existed and wanted to hire me for a job. [Now it is many years later and I am still looking for a job. I wish at the time I had taken that job. That's not the point.] So I said, "Wow! Thanks for thinking of me! What is the idea?"

And he said he would have his secretary send it to me if I would sign a nondisclosure secrecy policy.

And I said that was fine. But then I had a slight panic. What if I was sent the idea and I just couldn't write it? What would happen to me? I would be in trouble. So I told Mr. Krantz (that was his name), "I will read your idea with pleasure. But if I don't think I can write your television bible and pilot and series, is it okay if I just say no?"

"Of course!" he assured me. "There is no obligation. We would love you to do it, that's all, so just sign the nondisclosure secrecy statement, read it, and get back to me. I am going to give you my direct number, so you can call me directly."

A few days later I got the packet in the mail.

I opened the envelope. There was a twenty-page nondisclosure statement and the idea itself. The idea was: there are some women working on a magazine in New York City.

All they needed from me was the previously mentioned bible, plot, episodes, etc.

I thought for a long time and then it occurred to me: I don't want to write for television! I want to write novels and stories! I want to learn how to be a novelist and not a television writer! Also I was unable to do this job.

Not one idea based on his idea came into my head. I tried, for many days, but there was nothing I could think of. So I called him back on the direct number he had given me and his secretary put me through right away.

"Hi there!" he said. "You got the idea! You are all set!"

"I'm sorry," I said. "It is a good one, but I cannot do this project."

"What? What did you just say?"

"I can't!"

"You can't write this? Are you kidding me? I call you up, I give you this great opportunity and you say 'No'? Who do you think you are, anyway? Just who do you think you are talking to!?" It took him a long time to explain to me.

I was so scared. I started to cry. That's when Mr. Krantz told me that he personally would make sure I would never, ever write for television, and that I would never amount to anything or be anything. He had an extremely forceful way of explaining this to me and I was a very timid person.

I felt that my life was ruined, that he was right when he said I was a nothing, but I just could not think of anything about these women who worked on a magazine in New York City and led these glamorous lives.

Did they live in a basement so dark and damp that every time it rained mushrooms grew around the bottom of the toilet bowl?

example two

I always try to obey the law. One time, I was carrying my two-pound poodle to her vet appointment. She was in a pink snowsuit and I had her in a bag. I had to change from the express to the local train, and since I was running and didn't want her to be jostled, I took her out of the bag and held her in my arms while I ran across the platform and got onto the local train and sat down. The policeman entered the subway car and told me to step out. I got out. My dog was back in the bag.

"I have to issue you a ticket," he said. "It is illegal for dogs to be on the subway unless they are in a carrier."

"Oh, I'm sorry," I said. "I didn't want to jostle her. We are on the way to the veterinarian. She is blind and needs an emergency operation to have the eye removed. I did not want to be late."

"Don't worry," he said. "The train will be held in the station while I write you this ticket. What's your name?"

He wrote very slowly. The passengers on the local train began staring out at the policeman, who had been joined by two more cops, and at me, the perpetrator. The passengers looked restless.

There was a recorded audio announcement over the crackling speakers. "Due to a police investigation, this train is being held momentarily in the station!"

Now more passengers came to the windows.

"What is your address?" the cop asked me. He was very methodical and repeated the information. The announcement was repeated. Soon the passengers who were stuck began to appear hostile. "Don't worry," the cop said. "This train will leave but another will soon be here, in time to take you and your dog to the vet."

The train left. I got a ticket for twenty-five dollars, or if I preferred I could go to court.

I have seen many things on the subway. People spitting and eating and urinating. I have not seen tickets or summonses issued. I had broken the law by having a handheld poodle.

example three

When I was a kid, maybe ten, after my parents' divorce, I came up to my dad's house to assist him and his wife in organizing a splendid pig roast. I worked for days helping them get ready. When it was time for the party, guests began to arrive—children, adults, all ages of people. "Okay, you'd better go home now," Dad said.

"What?"

"You're not invited."

Apparently I was quite upset.

Years later someone posted about how difficult as a child I had been. The author had been a child who arrived at this pig roast and witnessed me having some sort of breakdown and being sent home. The author suggested that I was some sort of juvenile drama queen.

example four

When Willow was a baby, I took her to the bathroom to change her diaper. She was less than a couple of years old. In the lavatory a woman started to chat with me, asking me endless questions about the baby. When I got back to the table a man came over. He said he was an author and he wanted me to read his book. I suggested he mail it to me. That would not be necessary, he said.

He wanted me to take the manuscript right then and there. It was a large, bulky manuscript. I was in the middle of the meal, chatting with my friends, trying to enjoy my food. I took his manuscript, but I don't know what happened to it; we might have gone elsewhere that night, it might have gotten lost, I might have put it down at home and forgotten about it.

He printed an angry letter in the paper: he had seen me in the restaurant, sent his wife to delay me in the women's room while he ran home and got his manuscript, and gave it to me—only I was so rude I never responded.

the search for
help for willow

Days went by when I spoke to no one except the teenager. The teenager was sharp, smart, and charming, but she also knew she was living with a nincompoop. I knew that according to Mark Twain, when he was twenty, his father was the stupidest person on the planet, but when he got to be twenty-five his father got very smart. Willow was unhappy and she needed some advice but she didn't want advice from me. Against my better judgment I booked an appointment for her with the local psychiatrist of her choice, not the man with the hat but another who she had found, specializing in child psychiatry.

Willow was seventeen. She was in eleventh grade, and now she and I were living together, alone, in upstate New York. She was in high school here and every day I was going to see my mom in the nursing home and trying to pack up that thirty years of stuff in her house. I was trying my best, and my kid wanted to see a psychiatrist.

Sure, why not? If you hadn't grown up as the child of a psychiatrist, why wouldn't you want to see one? A kindly, sympathetic soul, interested in listening to you and exploring your issues? Willow researched online and found Dr. Leonid. She was proud of her discovery, so we booked an appointment. This guy was going to see her briefly, then he would meet with us both.

We went to his house, which was also his office. A woman sitting at a desk introduced herself as Mrs. Leonid; she was the doctor's wife, office manager, secretary, whatever. You have never met a more seriously depressed woman. Her aura—the atmosphere— reeked of potential suicide. The doctor came out, a small, wizened fellow with preternaturally bright and angry eyes, and we introduced ourselves.

He looked at me suspiciously. "Tama! I have never met a *Tama*."

"That's okay, I have never met a Doctor Leonid."

"Ha! Touché!"

He took Willow in.

A few minutes later I was called in.

"Sit down!" He is gleeful. "Did you know that your daughter smokes marijuana?" Willow winces. Maybe she wasn't expecting him to betray her, at least not so brutally, so immediately.

"Um, yes, I knew."

In my opinion, you might want to give a couple minutes' chit-chat before you break your patient's trust, but, whatever, you could see the disappointment in his eyes. "Your daughter is in serious need of psychiatric help! She is seriously depressed! She started crying when she came in here and she told me she cries every day!"

"Oh, so did I at her age. I cried every night."

"That's not normal! Your daughter is not normal!"

"Um, Dr. Leonid, do you have any daughters?"

"What?" A sizzling coil of rage, some kind of . . . I don't know, demonic entity? A dybbuk? He'd just shrunken in hate.

"Any daughters. Got any teenage daughters—or girls?"

". . . No."

"Do you have any sons?"

"No! But that's not the point. Your child says she hates school and she has ALWAYS hated school. I am going to prescribe major medication for her, antidepression, anti-anxiety, sleeping pills. BUT I WILL NOT GIVE HER THESE MEDICATIONS UNLESS SHE STOPS SMOKING MARIJUANA. Willow, will you do so?"

"Um, I don't think so."

"For today, the fee will be two hundred and fifty dollars. From now on I would like to see her four times a week at two hundred dollars a session. I will also need to see you, and Tim as well. Then after that, if necessary, any or all of you can call me—for fifteen minutes—and that is ninety dollars. Do you have any questions?"

"I have a question," said Willow. "What are your thoughts or opinions about the meaning of life?"

"For me?" He looked angry. "I am here to help people. That gives me pleasure."

We departed. I wrote a check and handed it to the depressed sodden mass of tissue that was the doctor's wife.

"Mom, I don't want to see that guy again," Willow said.

A short time later she got a boyfriend and a bicycle and didn't mention therapy again.

About six months later, Willow got this big-deal scholarship to learn Arabic in Jordan for the summer. It was very prestigious and had been a real bitch to get; letters of recommendation had to be obtained and interviews arranged and essays written. I was so proud and excited. She went to Washington, D.C., for two days of orientation. On Sunday night, when the group was scheduled to leave, first for Frankfurt and then on to Amman, the director of the program called and said, "Willow was crying, so we asked if she really wants to go on this trip and she said, 'No,' so we pulled her out and sent her to a hotel. She'll fly back to Ithaca tomorrow."

"What?" I said. "Where is she? Put her on the phone right now and I'll tell her to get on that plane with the group and shut her trap."

"Oh no," the director said. "The rest of the group is boarding and Willow has been sent back through security."

If there had been an issue, at least give me a chance to kick the child's behind and talk some sense into her; it was eight thirty and the flight was scheduled for nine. What could I do with that amount of time?

I could not stop crying. This scholarship would have meant her acceptance into college. The State Department offered internships and jobs to those kids. I had found her an Arabic tutor to assist her prior to the trip (the kids, all high school juniors and seniors, were supposed to teach themselves basic Arabic before the journey). I had bought presents for the host family she was staying with and got her a hijab, which, believe me, was not the easiest thing to find in upstate New York. Our neighborhood in Brooklyn would have been different. We had a lot of hijab shops, believe me, a subway stop or less away.

So I called the psychiatrist I'd seen before, Dr. Sandor F—. He had seemed . . . kind. I remembered he was expensive, and it had cost me a lot to hear his life story, but I was so upset I booked back-to-back appointments, one for Willow and one for me, the day after she got back.

Willow was back? I had had my summer planned: there would be house-sitters staying to look after my dogs. I would escape, after a year of total unending torture, a mom crapping all over the house and my having to find her a nursing home, and a kid who wanted to move to high school here and then found herself miserable because eleventh grade is not an easy year to switch schools and who then got a boyfriend to smoke pot with. After all that, now she was home only two days after she left. The scholarship to Jordan was a big deal! I took her to the shrink. When her appointment was over, I went in for mine. And the room . . . well, it smelled like pot. And Dr. Sandor F—, who I remembered as a nice guy, intelligent, on my one brief visit some six months prior, said, "I met with your daughter and I told her: 'WHY WOULD YOU WANT TO GO TO JORDAN! Those Arabs are crazy! They are bad people!'"

"Oh," I said.

"So why are you so upset?" he asked.

"This was a big-deal scholarship! She doesn't have very good grades or PSAT scores, it would help her get into college, they offer jobs to the recipients, blah-blah-blah."

"Okay, so I am going to tell you something," said Dr. Sandor F—. "It doesn't matter."

"Huh?"

"That's right, it doesn't MATTER." He launched into the history of cognitive behavior therapy, which I think he had told me before. This time the story went something like: "There was this very ugly guy, Eckhart Tolle, and he was so plain and ugly and he had no money and his parents were horrible. So you see, Willow not taking the scholarship—it doesn't matter. *She's* fine. *You* should come back for further appointments."

Right. It was true, he was right: it didn't matter. Nothing matters. But is that comforting? No. Not to me at the time. I understand you don't look to a psychiatrist for comfort, but still. Yes, sure, I would "get over it," but to me, it mattered.

"I am troubled by her marijuana smoking," I said. "She gets nasty after she hasn't smoked."

"And what is your problem with marijuana?"

I told him about my father, and how his long-term smoking had made him . . . if not addicted, then just unpleasant if he hadn't smoked in more than a few hours. "Look, if someone wants to smoke once in a while, it's not a problem!" I said. "But usage like that, it's no different than alcoholism. And even smoking once in a while, it's kind of like getting drunk, the people end up with hangovers!"

The doctor nodded thoughtfully. "I don't know anything about long-term usage like your father's," he says. "But in my opinion, it is not harmful."

So after my appointment I said to Willow, "Listen, were you smoking pot with that shrink?"

"No, why?"

"Just because . . . the place smelled like pot."

"Well, I wasn't," she said. "He seemed nice! He used to be a neurosurgeon. We talked a lot about brain function. And he said it would have been nuts to go to Jordan and that I didn't need to come to see him again. I'm fine."

A couple of weeks later, she was hanging out with her friends when she said, "You know what, Mom? I don't know why you are so upset with me smoking marijuana. There's this kid, at my school, Gandolf F—. He and his parents *grow* marijuana, in the yard, and they *smoke* it together. He started smoking when he was *seven*, with his parents."

"*What?* WHAT did you say his name was?"

She repeated it.

"That's the psychiatrist's son!" Not only was it an unusual last name, but Dr. Sandor F— had told me he had a kid in Willow's school. I was in total disbelief. I mean, Doctor—do what you want, smoke marijuana with your kid starting when he's seven years old, if you feel that's okay—but MAKE SURE you tell your kid to keep his mouth shut about doing it! You're a DOC-TOR, for crying out loud, it's your REPUTATION! Not to mention he previously worked for the state, so was he oblivious to the fact that anybody could call Child Protective Services . . . or the police . . . for growing marijuana? Were all these psychiatrists similar? When Willow was a toddler my dad wanted Tim to take a few pounds of marijuana he had grown, so Tim could sell it for him in the city. I forget what split he suggested.

"Dad!" I said. "Do you know what happens if you get caught dealing marijuana in that quantity? They don't just put you in jail—they take away everything you own, including your kid!"

Dad didn't care. Fortunately Tim didn't go through with this plan.

I was alone on this damn planet, not only suffering from repetition compulsion syndrome (or whatever it was called), I was out another $250 apiece for our appointments.

leaving ithaca

If I was going to look after my mother as her condition deterio-
rated and she got kicked out of one nursing home after the next,
each time demoted to a higher level of care, I would have to head to
a place where I didn't have neighbors, even if it meant abandoning
my shrub.

So this is how I actually got to Schuyler County, where they
had advertisements for events such as this:

A Holy Ghost tent revival *and* unlimited pizza buffet.

Yes, I would miss my shrub, and hearing things about my neighbor's biological daughter's grandfather's murder-suicide spree. Yes, I would miss many of the very wise recycling rules of Tompkins County and I would be sorry not to display my paper bags with fortitude to the garbagemen—by now I had learned to tape and strap them so well, they would last for thousands of years in the landfill. But it was time for me to go.

I was ready for Schuyler County, where—riding my horse through the Finger Lakes National Forest and surrounding farmlands—I could always find my way back to the farm, simply by remembering the various bathtubs that local residents had discarded along the trail. (Also, the horse knew the way.)

Bathtubs, sinks, sofas: if you had something you didn't want, that's what you did with it out there in the wild. And that was going to be my next destination, as long as my mother was on this earth, a place where seldom was heard the term *deer repellent*. Instead it was a realm where at the local convenience store you could buy deer *attractant*, made out of the urine of does in heat, in order to attract the male deer to shoot them while they were searching out the female deer in heat and distracted by the hormones in the scent. That was what fair play was considered to be in the region. And, in my opinion, it was just as fair as contacting a lawyer to tell your neighbor to remove a bag of mulch from the sidewalk.

At the end of the time I was in my mom's house I had been so scared of living there, with the legal threats and accusations and having to sit in a sex chair when I didn't want to. But then— just before I had everything 100 percent packed and gone—I was nervously cleaning up the yard, hoping I wasn't going to get the meditation command, when a car drove by on the far road and slowed.

At first I didn't know who it was, but then I saw, looking tired and peevish, a ponytailed guy, maybe in search of local overgrown shrubs or barking dogs, but anyway just weary, and it all made me a bit sad.

in search of lost time

Time passes, I end up there—that indefinable place called "Revisiting the Past."

It's not an accurate place. You can't go back and visit it in a documentary. Your mind doesn't remember it perfectly. You want to look back and think you did well. You want to believe people are basically good. You know, too, we all try to improve. We hope to change.

I find myself, once again, in that same supermarket.

Look, the sign has been changed!

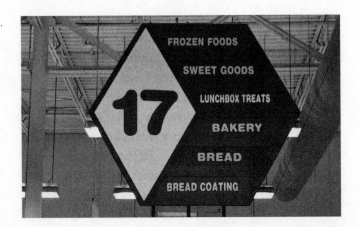

Oh no. It's changed, but it's not an *improvement*. Don't get me started. Don't get me started. So, in my head, I revisit. I revisit my time growing up. I revisit my life in New York: growing up—after my parents' divorce—in a tiny tract house, falling apart, alongside the big eight-lane highway 128 looping outside Boston. Rats in the back, neighbors throwing rocks at the car—once they broke my mom's windshield. It's a contagious disease, that place you came from.

Don't get me wrong; I did get to have plenty of fun, strange, and interesting experiences in my life. I did not particularly like being semi-famous, which I was for a while, after *Slaves of New York* was published in 1986.

The thing is, if you are a writer, and that's all you do, you have a pretty isolated existence. What experiences are you getting to have? You are sitting at a typewriter (well, to start, it was a manual, then a used electric, and finally a Mac) and that's your life.

Flannery O'Connor said that a writer has enough life experience to draw on by the time she is twenty years old to write for the rest of her life. She died when she was thirty-nine. The Brontës, they had plenty to write about, and they seldom left the moors.

But is that really a fun way to spend your life, all the time— unless you have to?

Writing, to me, was a living death. You are not "doing" anything while you are writing. You are not painting a picture or filing papers or trying a case. You are not in a meeting. You are sitting totally alone with a screen or paper in front of you and nothing is happening. You are making up stuff in your head, but that is not the same as something really "happening."

I did not write books to be liked. I was not interested in writing likable books. I was not interested in providing the reader with a hero or heroine with whom she or he could identify, who had to overcome obstacles and in the end triumphed. I wasn't writing about "nice" people or people who were redeemed.

I found rotten people to be more interesting. What made them the way they were? Thankfully, I found that even nice and decent human beings are pretty rotten as well.

I was in New York. I could take the subway and look at people. I could go to art openings. I could go to clubs. But it's still not easy to speak to people. I was always the observer, and it became harder and harder to leave my apartment. It was the same as a dog taken to an animal shelter and left in a cage for years. I couldn't make the transition out of my cage. And I was always so broke.

It wasn't fun being jeered at, when I started doing advertisements and that sort of thing—which I did, not only for the money, but for fun and experience. I looked upon any invitation to do anything as an opportunity to *do* something I would never have known about otherwise. For me, my activities were my substitutions. I could not be Hemingway, running with the bulls in Pamplona or fishing for marlin off Cuba.

I always had a sense of guilt, though. I mean, a writer in our society is looked down on, pretty much. If you tell people you are a writer, unless you can say your name is Stephen King, the first thing you will be asked—always with a certain patronizing sneer—is: "And have you published?"

"Yes."

"What's the name of your book?"

"Um, *American Dad*?"

"Never heard of it."

With my next book I was able to say, "*Slaves of New York*?"

But still, 99.9 percent of people could say, "Never heard of it."

It seemed like a joke to me when I went to movie premieres

and the photographers, lined up as you entered the theater, started shouting at me, "Tama! Tama! Look this way! Over here, Tama."

I wasn't a movie star. I wasn't trying to get my photograph taken. I wanted to slink in, unnoticed. Didn't they get it? *I was a writer!*

Thanks to my success, however, I got to see, do, and witness an astonishing number of things. I became friends with Paige Powell, who was at that time the advertising director of *Interview* magazine, and because of her I was invited to go on the Concorde to Sweden. Michel Roux was the first distributor of Absolut vodka in the United States, and by way of thanking *his* distributors he hired the Concorde and took about forty distributors and their spouses and a number of artists on this private trip.

Thanks to R. Couri Hay I got to take the *QE2*, first class, with my mother and Willow (who was then two) over to Southampton, giving a talk on the way.

With my cousin, Jeff Slonim, because we were both journalists, we took a blimp from Teterboro Airport around New York and over the city (the blimp was still allowed to fly over it then).

Magazines like *Blue* and *Vogue* and *Travel & Leisure* and *Food & Wine* (and many others) sent me to ride horses in India and climb Machu Picchu, drive a reindeer sleigh 450 miles north of the Arctic Circle (my reindeer ran off the path and into a bank of snow, knocking me off, then galloping for home, leaving me miles from anywhere in the wilderness as the temperature was falling) and a dude ranch in Wyoming. I went skiing in Sun Valley and Aspen, drove a Range Rover on the test course in Birmingham, England, and rode on a dogsled. I went to Egypt, the Atacama Desert in Chile, an exclusive resort in Anguilla. There was whale watching in the Victoria Straits, a hot-air balloon ride in Park City, swimming with pink dolphins in the Amazon. Literary festivals brought me to Australia, New Zealand, and Sweden. Germany, Canada, Belgium, Holland, and Spain.

I foraged for morel mushrooms in Idaho, picked cranberries in Oregon, went to Moscow pre-putsch. In 1973, while I was at the National Encampment for Citizenship, I'd visited the World Trade Center before it was finished—the top floor was a cement shell, through which the wind whipped; over the years there were parties up there, including one for me (to which I brought my dad, who was accosted by a baroness known for her predilection for S&M), and later, from our apartment in Brooklyn, I watched the second plane hit the tower and the buildings come down—before my eyes, while the same scene played on the TV.

I'll always remember this one: I was sent to interview a mob hit man in the Federal Witness Protection Program, in Austin, Alabama, who was now running for mayor.

When I got there, I couldn't get hold of him. He had been renamed by the Protection Program and was now called "John Johnson."

John Johnson's phone was busy for twenty-four hours. I was desperate. He had agreed to be interviewed. It was a farce; what kind of hit man in the Federal Witness Protection Program broke cover to run for mayor? But I had to get my story.

I assumed his phone was out of order. I didn't drive then, but even if I had, I was too scared to drive up to a hit man's house, un-invited. Then I came up with an idea: I would send him a telegram, saying I had arrived in Austin to interview him, as previously dis-cussed, but his phone didn't work.

But there weren't any more telegram companies. I called around. Western Union didn't do this anymore! It was before e-mail and texting, but there weren't telegrams anymore, not real ones. What was I going to do? Even though you couldn't send a real telegram, I saw there were still singing telegrams available.

So I called up the Gorilla-gram company. "Could you just go and deliver a message for me?"

"No. This is a singing telegram company. We can only go to someone to sing. What do you want us to sing?"

I had to make up a song for the gorilla to sing to the hit man. Better a gorilla than me!

The gorilla arrived at the hit man's house. John Johnson came to the door at last. The gorilla sang: "Hello, I am here in town / You said you would do the interview / Is your phone broken? Or just off the hook? / I can't get through to you."

John Johnson got really mad. The Gorilla-gram company called me and said, "Where did you send us? This guy threatened the gorilla!"

John Johnson called me right away, too. He was scary. "What the hell are you doing? I took my phone off the hook, I was tired from campaigning. Then I went out to do some work on my car, with my buddies, and you sent a gorilla. Are you nuts? I'm coming after you!"

He had decided he didn't want to be interviewed, but I had gotten my story, even if it wasn't the right one, exactly.

In my normal life back in New York City I lived in a 750-square-foot basement that was freezing cold in winter. In summer, when it grew too dry, a parade of slugs entered from the tiny back-yard. And there was an angry squirrel. It liked to come in and look for food. Sometimes I was there. Sometimes I wasn't. My dogs didn't care, but I was upset when the squirrel urinated and defecated on the pages of manuscript I had left on my typewriter.

There were a lot of fabulous times. Too bad I was afraid to enjoy most of them.

If I were going to live my life so far over again, the main thing

I would wish for would be not to be so scared: scared of getting in trouble, scared of being broke, scared that people would not like me. If I were going to do it over again, I would not care if I got rejected or I got bad reviews or someone didn't like me.

But I'm still broke now and it's hard not to be scared, even though I have spent a lifetime fighting it.

Because of my husband, Tim Hunt, who is so charming and outgoing and brilliant at times, I got to meet and make friends with all kinds of people in England, people I would never have met on my own; I stayed in castles, stately homes, and a farm in Brazil, and attended a million of New York City's most glamorous parties and events.

Because my book *Slaves of New York* was made into a film by Merchant Ivory, I got to be friends with James Ivory and Ismail Merchant and Ruth Prawer Jhabvala and travel around with Jim and Ismail doing promotion for that film, which was horribly reviewed in every city we went to, and only now is considered a gay classic and is screened often to sold-out audiences.

Because Tim and I adopted our baby from China, I got to have the best daughter on the planet.

The apartments and residences I got to see in New York City!

Apartments at the Dakota, with their huge gloomy rooms. Although Yoko Ono's place was all in white, which made it not so dark. Hers was staffed by people who had—years before—snuck onto the stairwell and hung out for days (obviously before security was upgraded) until they met John and Yoko, who befriended them and hired them to be butler and so forth.

There was Asher Edelman's apartment, an entire floor of a building occupying a block, done like a museum, room after room of massive paintings and sculpture. The ambassador from Liechtenstein, who lived on the seventy-third floor of a building not far from the UN, floor-to-ceiling glass with the city spread out on all sides, twinkling below. Jose and Mary Mugrabi's apartment, on Fifth Avenue, high in the sky, jutting over the avenue so the cars disappeared under your feet and reemerged on the other side. You could look out at the river of traffic or you could look at the Yves Klein and Warhols on the walls. Homes of artists—like Arman— that were entire buildings with elevators. Joan Rivers's apartment, which was the former ballroom of J. P. Morgan's house.

Diane von Furstenberg's studio: an entire building on, I think, Fourteenth, which was done up to resemble a sort of Turkish palazzo, all tiled and with a blue pool, very chic and "ethnic." She lived in the top floor of the Carlyle Hotel, several floors of penthouse; to get to one of the toilets you had to climb a flight of stairs even higher up. That toilet sat on the roof in its own glass box, looking over the city.

The biggest dwelling of all belonged to Bob Guccione. This man lived in a real mansion. I think eventually some Russian billionaire bought it. Bob Senior was having a birthday party for his son Bob Junior, who I knew. You couldn't believe there was a human being who got to live in this place. It took up a whole block. It was all stone, lined with bad Roman art. I don't know, maybe some of it was good Roman art, but the setting made it look Las Vegas fake. The whole place was dark and massive and stone. You were greeted at the door by bodyguards and tremendous Rhodesian Ridgebacks. It went on forever. My recollection for detail on this is not so great. The marble busts, the staircases, the endless dark and huge stone rooms and the indoor swimming pool. Atria, courtyards, whatever. I didn't get to see the whole house. Probably there are pictures of this somewhere.

You just kept looking around this place and thinking, this man made all this money by publishing pictures of vaginas.

swag and parties

My cousin Jeff Slonim once asked me, "Doesn't it bother you that people are nice to you now that you're famous?" And I said, "Not in the slightest, it's much better that they are nice."

I guess for some people who have always been rich or famous, people have always been nice to them. As far as I was concerned, people weren't very nice; and then, when I got a little famous, they got nicer.

I didn't care what their reason was.

I wasn't *very* famous, and I never got rich, but less than four years after I had moved to New York City, I was on the cover of *New York* magazine, posing in an evening gown in a meat locker next door to where I lived in the Meatpacking District, which back then was still a working neighborhood. And when that magazine came out, I was so excited I went and stood in front of a newsstand staring at that pile of magazines until a drunken derelict staggered up to me and knocked me over.

I was living in that former meat locker, measuring ten by thirteen feet, worrying every month: How am I going to pay the rent?

I didn't get money but I did get a lot of presents. And I was and am very appreciative of this. I think the presents I was given should be recorded. It wasn't like I was a movie star who is rich and gets paid a lot *and* gets tons of swag, constantly. If you are nominated for an Oscar, you get to go to a golden room before the event and pick out anything you want. But you already have so much money, you don't really appreciate or need those things. For me, it was different.

It didn't last long. But I got to be famous enough, briefly, that Orrefors gave me crystal champagne glasses, incredibly thin; Villeroy and Boch said if I attended their event I could pick out a thousand dollars' worth of their beautiful china. Montblanc gave me pens. When I went to the North Pole with Paige, she organized, through Columbia Sportswear, for us to receive warm boots. At perfume launches I was given bottles of perfume. Wonderful designers like Vivienne Tam and Lillian de Castelbajac (of Morgane Le Fay) and others gave me dresses and other clothing.

It was amazing!

The people who really would be thrilled for a lifetime are poor people. Like me.

I got invited to parties. Some of these parties, a half million or more must have been spent. There was a party for Russian Standard vodka where the vodka company owner rented the Statue of Liberty and the island and had boats take out guests to the place at night. There were luminaria set everywhere, huge Indian pillows to sit on, and bars with endless champagne and caviar and vodka. There were bands playing and you could climb to the top of the Statue of Liberty, which, at that time, wasn't even open to the public.

There were parties at the Guggenheim and the Whitney and in the Temple of Dendur and at the Museum of Modern Art. Parties for book launches and new corporations and jewelry. There were dinner parties in unfinished office towers, high at the top. There were lavish weddings at the Pierre. I wish I had kept a diary, because the parties said a lot about the times and the people.

BACK IN THE EIGHTIES I was lumped together with Jay and Bret, a couple of other young writers, and we were dubbed the Literary Brat Pack. Here's what we had in common: the fact that our books were not supposed to become big sellers and were never expected to get any attention, but actually *did*. They developed huge readerships among college kids, who went out and bought those three books and read them—not because they were assigned in a class, but for fun.

I knew each of my two packmates a bit.

I did get to meet many interesting people, though. Mentioning just a few, who have died: Joan Rivers, warm yet driven to achievement; Ismail Merchant; my brother-in-law the Formula One driver James Hunt, about whom the movie *Rush* was made and who was dark and brooding; Earl McGrath, a farm boy from Wisconsin who was president of the Rolling Stones' record company, then had an art gallery and was married to Camilla McGrath, a genuine Italian countess.

The half-French and half-American Princess Anne of Bavaria. Robert Mapplethorpe, David Bowie, Steven Sprouse. Larry Rivers, the painter who liked to talk about his youth and his love affair with his mom's armchair, into which he masturbated daily. Victor Hugo (with his deranged Hispanic accent, who was Halston's boyfriend), Fred Hughes (Andy's manager, who adored titled Brits most of all)—all kinds of lovers, loners, and other losers.

There was Ahmet Ertegun, hilarious and totally charming. How does the son of a Turkish diplomat end up being the hero—

the rescuer, the savior—of American rhythm and blues music? The vicious and clever poet-artist-critic Rene Ricard, mesmerizing and tricky as a rattler. And so many more.

You never get to be truly close to the characters in New York. The glimpses are fleeting; you meet people for dinner or at parties and events—for the most part they are not your colleagues or comrades or co-workers. You may not even like them. But all represent intensely burning stars that make up the galaxy of New York City, and when one dies the city is dimmed and diminished. And now I've come to realize, a lot of the time the people you really can't stand in the end are often the most memorable.

Which is awful, because the people you can't stand should be forgettable.

my new home

The Greek Revival house I bought was a simple, old upstate New York farmhouse, common to the region, filled to the ceiling with garbage, with broken walls and trees growing in through the porch. Inside were bloodstains and someone had scrawled in spray paint KILL MOM on the wall at the top of the stairs.

Every single room had fire damage and big holes cut in the floor, here and there, because obviously no one had ever been warm inside that house in 160 years. There had been attempts to install propane heaters, oil heaters, wood-burning stoves, potbelly pellet stoves, and electric heaters; there had been nothing but freezing cold people in there for all that time. The floors were rotten, the ceiling was broken, the walls were crumbling, there was the garbage.

It was my riding teacher, Stasia Newell, who had first told me about the property. She was, to me, a goddess, a guru, a Zen master. She didn't care whether anybody *liked* her or not! I spent my whole life wanting to be "liked," except in my writing. My writing, I wanted to be *unlikable*—but I even wanted to be liked for writing unlikable stuff.

Stasia was different. As I say, she didn't care if she was liked or not. For women, generally speaking, that attribute is what makes them leaders.

She walked like a panther on the face of this earth. She was hard and tough and rock-and-roll. She was androgynous and beautiful and unpretentious. She drove a tractor and could use a chain saw and could ride a horse on a hundred-mile endurance ride and do so elegantly. There was no more ferocious, exotic creature on the planet.

If only she weren't also a great salesperson, explaining to me how whoever lived in this house, right on the Finger Lakes National Forest, was going to be very happy there! How it would be in a family for generations and while the rest of the world got more and more built up, NO ONE could ever build up the place around here because it had the Finger Lakes National Forest on three sides. How it would always be a part of the beautiful forest.

I am not sure what else she said. I just knew I HAD to have that place. And, after all, it would have cost a hundred grand just to put my mom's rickety house back in some kind of shape.

No one had spent a dime on that farmhouse in at least thirty years, apart from cutting a new hole in the floor to attach to another heating system that didn't provide warmth. It couldn't be warmed, not when the windows were hundred-year-old nonthermal panes set in rotten wood frames, not when the walls were filled with straw and bits of paper that wasn't real insulation. There was a basement full of water and ancient dripping fiberglass put up by some previous inhabitant, which dangled uselessly to the floor.

When I emerged from looking over the place, Larry appeared—my soon-to-be new neighbor. He lived in the trailer up the road. He was dressed in an East German military mechanic's outfit, a one-piece jumpsuit. I think he had been wearing that since before the Berlin Wall came down, which may have been the last time he had seen another person. He was very sweet, but it had been a long time since he had spoken to another human being, and he needed to make up for all those years of silence. Remarkably, he was able to materialize every time I went out, holding a poem he had written for me. He had never been off Logan Road. He had lived with his mother until her death. Until our falling-out I had promised that some day I would take him to Walmart, where he had never been. His brother, with whom he lived in the trailer, had a truck—but this brother wouldn't give him a ride.

My offer was accepted for the 1850 farmhouse with forty acres surrounded on three sides by the Finger Lakes National Forest.

I saw it in July and got a contractor to look at it in August. The contractor was a local, grumpy, Kool-smoking guy—if you wanted to say that a guy who was hiring his sister and his sister's wife and his father to build my house was a contractor. He was, but to me, that made him a construction worker. A real contractor had a crew who weren't relatives.

But I hadn't closed on this house yet. I couldn't get the owner to complete the paperwork. The contractor kept telling me, "Look, if it wasn't for waiting for you to close, so I can get the work done while the weather is still good, I would be in the Adirondacks, I would be *hunting bear*."

I didn't want to lose the opportunity to have this man—highly recommended by Master Stasia Newell—renovate the house. So I was very anxious. Later I realized I was overreacting. Bear hunting season didn't even open for months.

The contractor said that while I was waiting for the property to close I should just come and live in his house. He called his home "the cabin." I was like, no, I was not going to go live with this contractor, but he kept mumbling that he lived with his girlfriend. She owned a year-round Christmas shop on the Glen, where the lake was located, specializing in elves, Norwegian sweaters, and hand-made velvet Christmas tree blankets, the kind that hide the base of the tree where it has been cut off and put in a stand full of water. (Although later I found out they weren't actually handmade—they were mass produced in a Christmas tree blanket factory in China and she cut off the labels and sewed on her own.) His home, "the cabin," was empty.

I asked my friend Sue Martin if she would come with me to go and look at it. The contractor was the sort of man who, for some reason, I didn't want to be alone with in a room, let alone a cabin.

He said it was only about ten minutes away from my "new" house, where he would be working, and from the farm where I leased a horse.

We got in his car to go see. We drove and drove. It was not ten minutes. We pulled in. From the road, it was a work facility, a barn with a tiny roof, one of those places you pass on the roadside. "This is it!" said the contractor.

"Twenty-three minutes," said Sue Martin, who was timing our drive.

The front side resembled a workspace, a factory. On the other side, it was a log cabin. He had built the roadside to look like a workplace. Around the back, it was High Adirondacks, skinned logs, a hot tub out on the upper deck—what anybody would prob-ably refer to as a testosterone palace. You've probably seen these places on TV, where real men live in Alaska. Inside, if it was indig-enous to North America and a man could kill it and have it stuffed, it was there.

There were stuffed and mounted trout and bass. There were stuffed and mounted turkeys. There were the heads of deer with antlers with few points and the heads of deer with antlers with many points. Fortunately there weren't any foxes, but there was a framed poster of a girl wearing a cowboy hat and skimpy shorts with her buttocks hanging out and the caption WIDE OPEN SPACES. I guess because she was looking out to the west.

"Wow," said Sue.

"Come in here," he said, and took me into the bathroom. There was a big shower, with large river stones lining the walls. "You could fit four people in this shower!" he said.

You could, too.

But why would you?

The whole place, it was great. It was authentic, it was real, I did like it. Don't get me wrong. If you took me into a 1500s farmhouse in Wiltshire, of daub, wattle, and thatched roof, with a large spit over the fire upon which be roasting a haunch, a loud beehive glade (you know the kind of place I'm talking about), it could not be more authentic. "So, you can live here," he said. "I ain't gonna be bothering you, I ain't around here. I'm living with my girlfriend, it's empty."

A few weeks passed and I was still down there, waiting for my "new" house to close. Closing on a house is something to do with contracts. It takes a long time as legal documents are prepared.

The contractor had gone over the whole place—with me, on his own—many times.

Every time I met him and he went over the property to give me an estimate, he sighed and shook his head. I didn't understand why, exactly.

I knew the place was kind of a mess. I knew maybe you would want stairs that you didn't fall through to get upstairs, and you would want things like a toilet and a sink. I just didn't know why having a place with walls that were falling down and floors that were buckling and broken windows signified any major issues.

Every time we arranged to meet and he went over the place and kept sighing, I kept sighing, too.

So, while the contractor viewed the property on which I had not yet closed and kept shaking his head, I kept sighing because he seemed to think it was going to be such a difficult task, fixing up this crumbling farmhouse.

He was a contractor, wasn't he? He knew how to do all that stuff.

Then I really screwed up. I fell in love with him.

He worked and worked and he stayed there, nights, while I slept in his warm man-cave cabin. And after a few months, even though it was a total gut renovation and he had had to rip out floors and rebuild them, and redo the wiring and the plumbing and the walls and the ceiling and the insulation and every single aspect, just like a house built from scratch, only more difficult, it looked like that house was ready for me to move into. From October to mid-December, that's how long it took him. It wasn't entirely finished, but he did a brilliant, elegant, very, very fine job.

I was innocent then. I did not understand that pipes had to be connected to other pipes and then to some kind of tank or pump in order to have water. I did not understand that you had to have wires going through the walls connected to a pole, or a generator, in order to get electricity. I did not understand.

I want to communicate. If you are reading this, and you have gotten this far in my memoirs, can you tell me how the elevator works if you are in an office, or the subway, if you had to take a subway to get to work, or your engine, if you drove a car? If you know, I am proud and happy for you.

Do you know how the key to your car is made? Where you put the transmission fluid? How your phone works? Let's say you are by your refrigerator, do you know about that coolant or whatever it is? I am sure you do.

But you are smarter than I. I don't get it. If there is a radio program, where does the sound go when it's over? Where does the image that comes out of your TV set go to, after the scene changes? What happens to the leftovers you toss from the vegetable bin? Where are the files you "deleted" from your computer? How do you use a sander? How do you level the ceiling?

Okay, I know—you know all this stuff.

But I don't! I don't understand.

My three months overlapped the right time. But the closing kept being postponed. I knew even once I had officially bought it, there would be months and months of additional renovation. That place was still not inhabitable. But for some reason, I just couldn't register these mathematical time-frame facts.

It was supposed to close the same day I sold my mom's house. It did not. My mom's house sold. I shipped the kid off to college, I put all the contents of my mom's house into storage. I had eight poodles and nowhere to go.

a trailer named esperanza

In all those years, my mother's colleagues from the university had never called me to see how I was doing. A couple might have visited my mom once. They never asked if I might want to teach a workshop at Cornell, or give a reading, or go to dinner. I know, people are busy.

But my new friend Sue Martin was different. She said if I had nowhere to go, I could live with her and her wife while the work was done on my new place. But I just couldn't inflict that on anyone that I wanted to stay friends with.

Sue found an ad for me on Craigslist. It was for an old trailer. The trailer was a 1966 silver thing; there was a picture of it in a field.

The woman was asking $450 a month, and I called her. She was in California. She said the trailer was named Esperanza and was in the middle of ten acres and it would be fine to go and live there with my dogs. I could live there until probably November, when it would get too cold. The place wasn't heated, but my dogs would be fine there and it would be a good place for a writer.

Anne had raised her daughter in the area, in a house next to Esperanza that was now rented out. Now she had moved to California, where she rescued seals.

She said she would have Esperanza's cistern filled with water and that it held a couple hundred gallons. She said she would get the propane turned on soon, and the electric. "And if you want to bathe," Anne said, "you can go for a swim in the lake. Or there's an old bathtub outside. If it rains, maybe it will fill up!"

I was slightly worried, but I was happy I had somewhere to go.

I put my eight poodles in the car and we drove the half hour to the trailer named Esperanza.

The trailer was in the middle of a field. It was a tiny trailer and the field was very sunny and very hot. I opened the door to the trailer. A wave of heat approximately 140 degrees swooshed out. Maybe it was more. I don't know.

Inside it was much less space than the picture had led me to believe. It had a built-in kitchenette table and banquette seats, there were twin built-in beds, but there was only a narrow space to get around in between the built-ins. I put the dog beds on the floor but that left even less space, especially after I moved my other things in.

It was already quite full.

There was a placard of wood on which stones had been glued that spelled ESPERANZA. There were forks and knives and mugs and a kettle and a lot of other stuff. I was surprised there was no water and there was no electricity, since I had thought, somehow, those things would be working by the time I arrived.

My friend Sue arrived and we managed to build an enclosure for my dogs, so that they would not have to sit inside Esperanza but wouldn't wander away in the unfamiliar field. Inside the trailer it was just as hot, even with the windows open.

The next day I went to the closing of my mom's house.

When I got near the turn-off for Esperanza, I noticed a lot of cars parked on the road, at the entrance to the next driveway. I guessed the neighbors in one of the nearby houses were having some sort of Labor Day Friday barbeque.

It looked like a big gathering. I might mosey over, I thought, when I had checked on the dogs and unloaded the water I had brought from the farm. The dogs ran out to greet me at the car and I was relieved they were alive. I stopped and I got out and I started to unload the nearly empty buckets. Then I realized: How did the dogs get to the car?

Sue and I had spent the entire day building a fence to contain them. Now I did a head-count. Candy Darling, Gertrude Stein, Petunia, Tartuffe, Moushka were here . . . but Demon, Fury, and Zizou were missing.

How had they escaped? I was exhausted. I wondered . . . perhaps the missing had gone to the barbeque down the road. I tried to fix the fence and push the remaining dogs back in, dousing the overheated ones with the water. Gertrude Stein in particular

looked kind of peaky. Then I headed out, shouting, "Zizou! Demon! Fury!"

There was a hedgerow separating the bottom of the dirt road
from the neighbors. I heard noise on the other side. "It's her! It
must be her! Hey, cut it out!" It sounded like some kind of struggle or altercation was taking place, and Demon—the larger white
poodle—crashed through the bushes and came bounding to me.
"Demon!" I said. I got to the road. Fury was running in circles as if
he was being chased, but when he saw me he stopped and I picked
him up. He weighed three pounds. Now a lot of people came running toward me. It was a lynch mob.

"YOU!" a woman shouted.

"It's her!" others yelled. "Get her!"

"Are you the owner of these dogs?"

"Yes," I said. "My dogs escaped, I'm still looking for Zizou!"

"I have him—in a cage!" the woman said. "Do you know what
happened? Do you know what you did? Your dogs escaped! They
ran into Searsburg Road. *How many dogs do you have!?* They could
have been killed! I stopped. I had to shut down traffic! All these
cars stopped!"

She pointed to the other six vehicles. There had been more, but
they were gone by now. "Luckily, I had a cage!" She pointed to a
tiny box. I went over to it. The woman tried to take it from me, but
I got there first. My dog Zizou exploded from the confines.

"We didn't know where these dogs came from!" a man shouted
as he shuffled toward me. "They came from everywhere. We didn't
know where they were coming from. Some were here and we tried
to catch them but they escaped that way." He pointed up the dirt
road to the trailer.

The other people looked very angry. "Yes, we tried to catch

them!" They began to stumble toward me ominously. "We have been delayed because of this event."

"I called Animal Control!" the woman screamed.

"I'm so sorry! I just moved into the trailer. I tried to make a fence but they got out. I had to go to get water."

Zizou was panting. "That dog has respiratory problems!" the woman said. "I know dogs. He is sick! He needs veterinary care. Animal Control is coming! These dogs could have been killed! I called the police."

"Thank you so much," I said again. "I'm so embarrassed. I'm terribly sorry."

The people got back into their cars and I walked with Demon and Zizou and Fury the few hundred feet back to the trailer. It was afternoon and very hot. I yelled at the dogs for a while.

A man crashed through the brush on the far side of the field. He looked angry. There sure were a lot of people around, even though it had seemed, at first, this trailer was in the middle of nowhere. "Sorry!" I said. "If it was about my dogs escaping, I fixed the fence, I hope."

"Are you living here now?" he said.

"Temporarily."

"Who said you could live here?"

"The owner."

"No. You can't stay here!" he said. "She had no right to let you stay here. You can't stay here! You do not have a septic system! I am calling the Board of Health. You have to leave."

He disappeared back through the shrubs.

I went to the porch. I sat down for a minute on the chair I had brought. It was early evening now, but still just as hot.

A police car drove up. A cop got out.

"Hi," I said.

"Somebody called and reported your dogs got out," he said.

I was filled with terror. I was overtired and dehydrated. I started to cry. "Are you Animal Control?"

"No, I'm the police. I don't know if Animal Control is also coming."

"Will I be arrested?" I said.

"What?" he said. "Do your dogs have licenses?"

"What?" I said. "No. Am I going to get a ticket? I'm going to jail?"

I couldn't stop crying. I tried to calm down. In prison I would have running water. I could shower. Even my dogs would be better off. When Animal Control came, they would be taken to a kennel, or to the pound.

What was I doing here in this trailer? Why was I here? I had spent years moving my mom from nursing home to nursing home, driving miles to visit her. I had spent years cleaning out her house, getting her things packed, trying to stop her house from falling down. I was totally alone. "Take me," I said to the officer, and I put out my hands to be cuffed.

"I don't know why they called the police," the cop said at last, and he left.

I was hungry and hot and sticky and I hadn't obtained any provisions for myself, but I fed my dogs and we all piled into the trailer and I shut and locked the door. It was too hot, really, to sleep with the door shut, but by now I was awfully jittery.

In the morning the owner called my cell phone. "How's it going?" she said.

"There's no electricity. There's no water. There's no propane. I am in a tin can with my dogs and nothing works."

"I'll send help," she said. After a few hours a truck turned onto the dirt road and a man got out. "I'm a friend of Anne's," he said. "She said you needed help."

The man was very angry. "It's Saturday," he said. "It's Labor Day."

He fiddled with the equipment for a long time. "Even if the electricity was working, the pipes in this thing are ancient!" he said. "There is no way to get the water running through them."

He tried to get the propane to work. He poked and prodded and he flipped a switch and there was a crackling noise and then a loud boom. "Get back!" he yelled. A big cloud of black smoke started pouring out. "Get out now! It's not safe!"

I grabbed a few things and I put my dogs in the car and drove to my friend Sue's basement in Ithaca.

It wasn't really a basement; it had sliding doors to the outside. It was a normal house. There was water, and a washing machine and dryer. In the evenings I would go upstairs. I cooked vegan food for Sue. Kristine, Sue's wife, was vegetarian, so she liked the food, too. Sometimes I would watch TV with them. My dogs only escaped once or twice, at the beginning, then the neighbors appeared, but they were not irate or enraged the way they had been in the neighborhood of the trailer. I sat in bed every night with my poodles. I never knew before that how happy I could be.

I'm sitting on the couch upstairs in Sue and Kristine's house when the contractor stops over one night to see me. He pulls up the drive, he's dressed in his work boots and tight jeans and hoodie, and the four of us are hanging out, when Devin, their daughter, comes in. She's just arrived home from Maryland for a couple of days. She stops in the doorway for half a second, startled. I keep thinking of that movie *La Cage aux Folles*, only this is the opposite?

Here she grew up in this normal home with two vegetarian moms and a younger brother, gets back from college for a few days, and a middle-aged woman has moved into the basement with eight poodles and her parents are entertaining a tattooed, mustached Kool-smoking guy with a big truck parked in front of the house. Then she takes off her shoes and sits as if it's all perfectly usual. Now the scene was pretty much like a face-off: the Indigo Girls versus Ted Nugent.

A few weeks went by and I was telling someone about Esperanza, and how that trailer blew up when the man tried to turn on the electricity and how my eight poodles escaped and the police came. And there was something very familiar about this story, not just because I had told it a number of times. I was uneasy suddenly.

Then I remembered: some years before I had written a book, *By the Shores of Gitchee Gumee*. In this book, the family lived in a trailer with eight dogs and the dogs escaped and the police came and then the whole trailer blew up due to a propane tank incident.

There were a few differences between what had happened to me and the family in this book I had written so many years previously. For example, the family owned eight Mexican hairless dogs (xoloitzcuintlis), *not* poodles. And the family consisted of a mother and five kids—each by a different father. Then the mother ran off and ended up living with another woman in California as a lesbian. And when the trailer in the book blew up, it slipped down the hill and into the lake below.

Esperanza, the trailer, was in a flat field, although it's true Cayuga Lake was only a short distance away.

Still, there were plenty of similarities. But I had forgotten all about it, pretty much, even though they had—a few years before—made this book into a film.

It was a really big production, a major picture, and it was in Russian.

Part of the movie was filmed in Crimea, on the Black Sea. So they flew me over to see the shoot. I took Willow, who was about eight at the time, and my mom.

We flew to Kiev, then we had to change airports, I think, and then fly to Crimea, and then get to the odd, remote hotel in the dead of night and wake up the manager to take us to a room.

A driver from the movie crew took us in a van the next day three or four hours to the location. There, we were given a cottage. We wandered down to the set. On the beach, they had blown up the trailer the day before.

Actually, it wasn't really a trailer. The book had been altered to star Russian actors, and the Russians didn't live in trailers. They had built—for the film—a beach house on stilts and blown that up. It was in the book: the little boy had turned on the propane stove and it blew the place up.

We missed the big explosion scene by one day; the set was just a huge heap of rubble on a beach on the Black Sea. I was wearing a big beach hat and my mother was wrapped in some kind of blanket because she was cold, and Willow had on her own costume, a giant flared skirt from Chile, I think, or whatever else she had deemed suitable, since I would never argue with anyone about his or her choice of clothing.

We stood looking at the disaster zone for a minute, and everyone on the shoot—the cameramen, the director of photography, the lighting people, the sound guys, the hair and makeup artists, the actors—stopped to stare.

Finally someone came over. "Excuse me," she said in Russian. "Can I help you?" Of course I didn't know what she was saying, but she got someone over who spoke English. It turned out, I was later told, that when the three of us arrived on the beach, the whole crew had just quit what they were doing to stare because, as one person said, "Who the hell are those people? They look like materialized characters out of the film!"

After they figured out who we were, though, they were friendly. My mom started muttering. "Oh, there's a Chinese crested! It's Lily."

I looked around. There was no Chinese crested dog, let alone my mom's deceased Chinese crested, who was named Lily. "No, Ma," I said. "Are you okay? There's no way you would find a Chinese crested in Crimea."

I just didn't know what to do. Was this a sign that my mother was developing dementia? It had been a struggle, getting her on the campus-to-campus bus from Ithaca and then to Brooklyn on the subway and then to Crimea, but that was because her legs hurt. Maybe the trip had been too much for her?

They were filming this dude—he looked kind of like Joe Dallesandro from an Andy Warhol/Paul Morrissey film—as he came out from under a broken wreck of a car on one of those dollies the mechanics lie on. He had a big spliff in his mouth.

It was a really great scene, I had always loved Andy Warhol's films and I was just so happy that they were making a film like this.

I had totally forgotten, it was in my book.

Then they shot another scene. They brought out a Chinese crested dog. It looked just like my mom's dog, Lily. Only it was named Lula. They took this dog and they put it on a couch that was floating in the Black Sea. Then the actor who looked kind of like Joe Dallesandro dove into the water and rescued that dog from the sofa. That was the dog my mother had seen earlier, which was whisked off the set, leading to my idea she had dementia.

Do you see why I am so confused? In my book—which I had forgotten—one of the family's xoloitzcuintlis had gotten tossed into the water in the explosion and one of the boys in the family, who looked like Joe Dallesandro, who wanted to be an actor, dove into the lake to rescue it.

To recap: the original book had EIGHT Mexican hairless/ xoloitzcuintli dogs.

The Russian movie did not have xolos but did have ONE Chinese crested, which *was* a dog that I had had.

I actually had two, but I ended up giving one, Lily, to my mom. My mom used to take that dog to her office at Cornell, and then to teach class with her. Lily had her own chair at the seminar table.

I still can't make sense out of what I am doing with my life, let alone what happened.

The trailer Esperanza blew up years *after* I wrote my book. It was years *after* the movie shoot. I had eight poodles. The police came. I did not fall in love with the cop the way the girl did in the book.

But they made a really great Russian film from it.

1850

tried to do the research on my new place. I obtained things like
diaries of people's lives in the area:

A farmer in the 1900s had to do many things by hand that
are mechanized now and he made or devised tools and imple-
ments he could not readily acquire. Among the many things
Fred mentioned doing are rewooding a tackle block, solder-
ing a milk can, making whiffletrees and a 25-foot pole lad-
der, constructing a stone boat and a wire stretcher to string
fence. . . .

He slaughtered his hogs himself until one bit him and
thereafter had Lawrence McCarthy the butcher do it for
30 cents and later 50 cents each. He smoked some of the meat,
cut up and put some in brine, and made some into sausage.

(from Mecklenburg Farm Life 1905–1919, *compiled from the
diaries of Fred Dickens and Harriet Kennedy Dickens, by Shirley
Dee Taber Watt)*

For more information, I went to the Schuyler County Clerk's Office. This is located in a large brick courthouse in the center of Watkins Glen. It's got everything in it: the city court, the DMV, I don't know, a lot of social services, and you have to go through a metal detector right beside the only UPS pickup in town—it gets picked up once a day at three, and if you have a UPS package that is small and flat, you can ship it here, otherwise, you have to go for, like, twenty miles to find a UPS or FedEx office.

So you go to this room, the county clerk's office, and they will explain to you what to do. There's a room with books in it. You can go there and you can look up the previous sale of your house. It is not done on computer. You go there and you pull books off the shelf. You first go to one book and it has the name of the owner who sold it to you, and it has the name of who they bought it from, and some numbers, which you go to another book on another shelf to look up the one prior to that.

I got a lot of these deeds of previous owners, going back to about 1884, before I gave up. I couldn't figure out how to retrieve the previous owner information.

The deeds said things like:

THAT TRACT OR PARCEL OF LAND, situate in the Town of Hector, County of Schuyler and the State of New York, bounded and described as follows: BEGINNING at the Southwest corner of the farm now owned by parties of the first part (the Miller Farm) and a short distance Westerly of the Logan Road; then North 06 55 19 East a distance of 2,650.68 feet along the Westerly line of the said Miller Farm, the Northerly portion of which line is designated by a fence and hedge row to a steel pin designating the Northwesterly part . . .

It didn't seem like any owner had ever been able to hang on to the place for more than thirty years. Whatever. I'm telling you, it COULD be interesting to someone.

I couldn't focus, though. A man came back there. He had a long gray beard, missing teeth, and overalls. The county clerk was bent over one of the big books, looking up something.

"Hey!" the man said. "Psst! Hey! I got some tomatoes in the back of the truck. You wanna buy some?"

He acted kind of guilty and seemed suspicious. I don't know where he got those tomatoes.

The county clerk said, "What kind of tomatoes?"

"Small ones."

"How much are they?"

"Five dollars."

"I don't have any money on me right now," the county clerk said.

It was the time of year before the tomatoes were ready locally and I am guessing the man might have had a greenhouse. Or maybe they fell off the back of a truck.

In Brooklyn, when we first moved there, the neighborhood was rough. There were no restaurants. Tim went out to the Arab bodega. A guy comes over to him. "You look like you are new around here!" he said. "Here's my cell phone. You want marijuana, I will deliver."

You couldn't get anything to eat, but you could get home delivery of marijuana.

I knew my old 'hood back in Brooklyn. Now I knew where to score tomatoes off season in Watkins Glen.

I gave up on researching the house. It was just so much more interesting that there was a tomato dealer in the county clerk's office of the courthouse than who had struggled to live in my house before me.

another day, another nursing home

Mom's newest nursing home was a hospital wing. It was clean and had a beautiful view, but it was as bleak as you can get.

In the previous places, there was always some activity taking place: students playing the violin and flute or belly-dancing even though no one could get out of a chair. They had a strange man who came in and talked to them about funerals he had attended. A nurse brought her horses into the atrium.

This was not a Jewish area. This was not a people-of-color area.

Still, those Christians did have things they provided for occupational therapy, like giving the inmates Cheerios and glue and food coloring to make pictures on paper plates. And there were always piles of washcloths, tea towels, and napkins to fold.

The new home, in the local hospital, was only fifteen minutes away from my new house. I had been driving forty minutes to an hour each way before this. Here, there was a spectacular view of Seneca Lake. There didn't seem to be many activities, though. One day I saw a lecture was being giving in the dining hall. Finally, something my mom could listen to! I wheeled her in. There were about ten people in the room. There was a slide show taking place.

The pictures were of marginally alive, naked and beaten, emaciated Holocaust victims.

The man giving the lecture was standing at a podium with his computer. He looked angry that I had come in, wheeling my mother. "We are having a show and lecture on the Holocaust!" he said, like I was intruding.

I wasn't going to stick around to try to figure out why. "Okay!" I said. I wheeled her out.

That nursing home cost $10,500 a month. Fortunately my mom still had some long-term health insurance coverage left. It was running out fast, though. After it did, any money she had was going to pay for this. "Look, Mom," I said, "what if I build a little house for you, on the property where I'm living? You will be in the country. It will have a view. I will be there for all the meals. I will sleep there at night. I will get you a hospital bed and I will get staff for the day—and it will still be cheaper than if you stayed here. And we will watch TV at night and the dogs will be with us."

"Great!" my mom said. "When will it be done?" These were the first coherent words she had said to me in a long time.

Initially I had thought there would be a way to make the Greek Revival farmhouse accommodate her needs. But by now, she was going to need a special shower to bathe, a bigger wheelchair, a hoist, wider doors. She needed full-time care; she could not turn over now. So I discussed it with the contractor. And he said he would be able to build a small house for my mom, right next to mine. And he would build it for a hundred thousand dollars.

At night we drew sketches. It was fun, lying around in bed, drawing and trying to explain what kind of roof I wanted on the place, showing him pictures of Japanese houses and Chinese houses, because I didn't just want your local tract/ranch house and I didn't want your local log cabin place . . . if I was going to have my mom in a tiny house, I wanted something aesthetically pleasing. But I knew I didn't want a "modern" house here, or a glass house, because it was going to be too jarring to look at, right next to my Greek Revival.

I just couldn't seem to communicate what I wanted, though, until one day he said, "Git in the car," and he drove me to the abandoned train station. And I loved it. I had driven past this station hundreds of times and never paid any attention to it, but the contractor—he had noticed it, and now, from his looking at pictures of old Japanese houses with disbelief, it turned out he knew exactly what I was trying to say.

If there was a building like this next to my house it would look like, maybe, once there had been a train station here.

Then he found out: a structure for human habitation, larger than five hundred square feet, needed to have an architect's stamped set of plans. So he went in the Dandy one day. The Dandy was the local gas station, where you could buy stale chips and devices to lure turkeys. Sooner or later everybody bumped into everybody there. He asked a woman who worked there, "Say, do you know any cheap local architects?" and she gave him a guy's name.

I was to meet the contractor at the architect's house. The architect lived in one of those big old houses in downtown Ithaca, a large innocuous house maybe from the early part of the 1900s, stucco, on a very tiny piece of property surrounded by other houses. The contractor was already there, in the big truck, waiting for me on the curb. And so I went and knocked on the architect's door.

When he answered, he didn't seem to know why I was there. He looked right through me. He didn't ask my name or who I was. He said the contractor should sit on the porch. He didn't offer water, although it was a hot day. He was a very tall, bony man, like a stork or some other wading bird, slightly hunched and uncomfortable. We sat on his porch and then he said to the contractor, "Well, what is this place you are building *for*?"

"It's a house." The contractor showed him the sketches and drawings.

The architect began to shout. "You said you had plans already! These are not plans! These are nothing! Nothing!"

It was alarming. And the contractor said, "Well, they have all the specifications on them. The one thing I had trouble with was the roof."

And the architect got more upset. "You told me on the phone

you were coming to me with plans for the house. These are not plans. You said you wanted to hire me for ten hours of work—this is going to be twenty hours of work! Why would I do this project?"

The contractor tried to calm him down a bit and smooth his feathers.

Finally the architect agreed he would take another look at the drawings. "Why would you have a door here?" He got irate all over again.

"It's for a person in a wheelchair," I said.

"What?" Before, the architect hadn't seemed to acknowledge my existence. He didn't say, "And how are you associated or involved with this project?" Maybe he thought I was just the contractor's girlfriend, I don't know, but it was still odd.

Maybe by now I was invisible. You know, there is a whole percentage of the population of the United States who are invisible. They are the middle-aged women with fluffy gray hair. They are the women who get ignored, waiting on line or in an office waiting room. They are the women who try to be kind and good and decent and dress nicely, and because of that they become invisible.

My hair wasn't gray, but there is still this veil of invisibility that gets tossed over a lot of women.

Now he suddenly registered my existence. "You didn't tell me this was going to be a structure for someone who is handicapped! What is *wrong* with this person? I was not told this was a project for someone who was sick!"

"It's my mom," I said.

"You will be stuck with a back door in this house when she is able to walk!"

"She's not going to be walking again."

"She will never get up again? She will get better at some point!"

"No."

"No? Oh really, please. Cut it out. . . . And you can't have a door in a bedroom."

"I can't have a door in a bedroom? How do people get into their bedrooms?" I said.

He let out a squawk. "I mean a door to the outside, in a bedroom! That's terrible. And these windows! Look at these windows, why do you need all these windows?" He took a pencil and began to sketch, making a picture of a house without windows. "You don't want windows or doors in a bedroom, you want privacy!"

"But I want doors in a bedroom. French doors."

"No!" he was livid. "Maybe sliding glass doors, but not French doors. What kind of curtains are you going to have?"

"I don't know!" I said. "Venetian? Venetian . . . blinds?"

"Who's going to clean them? Do you know how difficult that is, to clean venetian blinds?"

"Okay—regular curtains? Maybe with little flowers?"

"Um, it's the roof we need help with," the contractor said grimly. "The company I use doesn't build trusses like these."

"I don't understand. What are you possibly thinking you are doing with the design of the roof?"

"It's . . . we want it . . . it's supposed to be like an old train station."

"You know the train station in Burdett?" I said.

The architect's bird eyes softened for a moment. "Yes," he said.

"You do?" I was surprised.

"I know it," said the architect, and he drew a roof. It wasn't really like the roof of the train station in Burdett, but I was so surprised he knew this abandoned train station in Burdett, and that he had suddenly stopped shouting, that I nodded at his sketches and said, "Oh, great."

Finally the architect calmed down enough to agree to draw the plans for the house, and we agreed that we would pay him for twenty hours, and the contractor gave him a "retainer" for a thousand dollars that would be refundable. Even though by now the architect must have figured out that I was the client, he still didn't speak to me or look at me when we left.

The contractor and I went and got a bite to eat. "I don't understand," I said. "Where did you find this guy? I never met someone who hates windows so much!"

"I was in the Dandy. I asked for the name of a local architect. He grew up in Burdett. He designed the Dandy. And you know that building in the center of town?"

"You mean the really ugly one?"

"Yes."

"The one that looks like a cement chicken coop? With a base of crushed brick? The one without any windows?"

"Um . . . yes. That's the library."

"Why didn't you tell me! That's the most hideous wreck anywhere. I thought it was a prison."

"It was a beautiful old grange. The architect inherited it and rebuilt it."

Every week that architect sent another bill. By the time he was done he had billed for forty hours, and at every meeting he screamed. He wouldn't return the escrow or retainer. He handed in plans that made no sense. But at least we had the plans, and the contractor was able to redesign it.

The contractor added black walnut trim, and windows and doors and anything else you see on it that made it special. He made counters and beams and a mantelpiece and it was a combination of Japanese and whimsical and graceful. You would not think someone who had hands like slabs of meat and did not read books and was angry and powerful could have such wonderful visions. But he did.

Then, Mom died. I had only gotten to show her pictures of it in progress.

goodbye

I was at the Chemung County Fair when it happened. I had gone to watch the contractor's sister Suzette play in a horseshoe tournament. I knew nothing about horseshoes before then. Sometimes at a family gathering, my dad and his uncles and his cousins might play, but I never quite got it myself. It turned out this was a very big sport, especially in upstate New York. And the contractor's sister was very good at throwing those horseshoes. I went to watch her qualify for the state championships in Montour Falls, at the Moose Lodge.

I had passed the Moose Lodge many times. It was a large, nondescript, tin-roofed structure with a big sign in front announcing the dinner menu; once in a while the sign would say it was open to the public, but even so, the food advertised was never really very appealing.

Horseshoes wasn't the most photogenic or charismatic of sports. The players were, generally speaking, dressed in grubby T-shirts and, for the most part, not physically beautiful specimens. Horseshoes lacked the visuals to become a commercially supported activity. There were no players in tight little outfits whacking balls back and forth, or Argentinians galloping on horses, or men on skates speeding around and bashing each other.

You could see that this was a complicated and difficult sport but was not going to get many sponsors, and this was probably why there were only a few people sitting around watching in the side lot of the Moose Lodge.

Even bowling had more visual drama than this. But I sat next to a man in his sixties named Spike who had a lot of big tattoos and a mustache. One of his tattoos was of his two-year-old granddaughter, who had been killed when someone backed their car over her, then drove off and tried to pretend it never happened, but got caught. Spike started crying, and he wasn't drinking beer, either. He had had polio, so one of his feet was in a very large shoe. He was really nice. I couldn't help it, I just liked sitting next to this handsome guy in a baseball cap with a clubfoot.

I could be "one" with the people. I had lived in a trailer, even if it was for only two days. The workers the contractor knew, or met, and put to work on the project, were so stoned all the time they walked around in a cloud of smoke. You could literally see it, I am not exaggerating—it was like Pigpen from *Peanuts*. They mostly had no teeth. They were on Social Security disability, so the contractor paid them under the table or they would get their SSI checks rescinded.

They had the bleak haunted look of men who had never eaten anything outside of the hamburger, mayonnaise, and Dorito food categories. They had long straggly hair and beards, and with the teeth missing, they could have been twenty-five or seventy-five— but they all looked seventy-five. These men, with their gnarled, gaunt faces and their wide, stark eyes, they were all as interesting to me—or more interesting!—than the "sculptors" and "artists" and "actors" in New York hustling and jockeying for position and trying to impress you with what restaurant they had eaten at or who was showing their work or what movies they were going to be in.

These men were broke, they were crippled, they were angry, they were stoned, they were illiterate—we did not have the same references, even though we probably had all watched the same TV shows. They were as foreign to me and as strange and as inscrutable as if I were in another country.

So now I was at the Chemung County Fair and Suzette was playing this horseshoe tournament. It was a big fair and it was a good fair because it did not just have a midway with rides and fried items, it had a big building with the horticultural displays, where there was table after table where people had brought in bouquets of, say, their roses or gladiolas, or their flower arrangements, most of which were now dying or wilting because it was the last day of the fair, and things they had knit or crocheted, like socks and blankets and stuffed bears, and jars of pickles, all of which I found very fascinating.

There was another barn with rabbits that were being *judged*, and another shed with pigs. I think some of the pigs were going to be sent to be slaughtered after the fair, because there were children in a few of the pens lying on top of their pigs, sobbing gently.

Even though the contractor was acting kind of cold to me, it was still a happy day. I bought some kind of fried dough thing for the contractor's beautiful mother, Sylvia, who was there watching Suzette play, and I thought, it is so great to be with people, especially women, who actually eat a big fried dough thing, because where I came from, the most any woman ever ate in New York City was a leaf—with the dressing on the side.

As I was giving her this dough thing dripping with oil and cinnamon-sugar on a paper plate, I saw I had gotten a phone call from the nursing home. It had come in a few minutes earlier. I hadn't heard it; maybe I was looking at the gladiolas.

I called back. The woman said, "Just a minute," and then another person got on the phone and said nonchalantly, "Hi, Tama. Your mother died at lunch about a half hour ago! When do you think you'll be able to have her body picked up?"

I sat down on the grass. I had seen my mom the day before. She had been kind of out of it, for her. She was in some kind of big reclining wheelchair but she seemed to be watching TV. I'd sat with her for a bit and had planned to go back that afternoon, after the horseshoes. I lost it and started crying and crying; Sylvia and April, Suzette's wife, were hugging me and trying to talk to me, but . . . I was in shock.

My mother! My mother was dead? There was nothing wrong with my mom! I was getting a little cottage built for her, on my property. My mother had said, "Yes, please! Great! When will you get me out of here?" and I had put ads in the papers to try to find staff to take care of her; it was a big project but her little house was almost complete and we were going to be together. Because my mom was my friend—she was my best friend.

She had always been my best friend. Yes, she could be difficult. She could go into a black rage and slam a door and not speak to me for three days. It didn't matter. She had always been my friend. We spoke every day, for a long time. She knew my entire life, she told me I was great, she helped me with my writing, she was brilliant, she was kind, she was supportive, there was no one else on the planet who cared for me like my mom did.

Sylvia and April were so sympathetic, and I was crying, "My mother, my mother." And then I was saying, "And the contractor doesn't love me, he doesn't care about me." And at that moment I just thought if he cared about me, I would not be alone on this planet. But he didn't care about me. He had not even come to see his own sister qualifying in this important match. I had my venomous brother and I had my insane father. I sat on the grass and bawled and bawled.

remembering andy

In 1987, I was in Princeton, New Jersey, when the phone rang. It was a former journalist I knew in New York City, who had once written an article about me for the cover of *New York* magazine. It was all a fluke, getting that cover story. The journalist had asked to borrow my letters for the piece, saying she just wanted to read them and that she would return them to me. She never did.

Now she called to say, "Did you know Andy Warhol is dead?"

"What?" I said, shocked.

She told me that that morning Fred Hughes, who was Andy's "business manager," had called Ed Hayes, a lawyer, and said, "Andy is dead, will you come to his estate?" So Ed Hayes immediately called a reporter for a New York newspaper. It was his job to keep things private, and he was on the phone calling the tabloids. But that wasn't the point. Before this call, I hadn't even known Andy was in the hospital. I had seen him a couple of nights before at some opening, and he had told me he was going to be modeling that night in a fashion show, but I didn't feel like going.

Andy had told only one person he would be in the hospital,

because, ever since he got shot in the 1960s, he had an obsessive fear of dying in a hospital.

I called Paige, Andy's and my mutual friend. "Paige, I got a call that Andy died."

"What?" she said. "No, of course not. You're wrong."

But she called me back a minute later. "Oh, Tama," she said. "Come quickly."

I got the train to New York City and went to her house. It was awful. She had told me that the nurse had been asleep while Andy filled with fluids; and then, too, maybe it was something his doctor had done incorrectly. Years later, this doctor died in a horrible way, some kind of event had happened and it was apparently while engaging in some kind of rough sex, and he was badly burned and was found stumbling down a street in Manhattan. I don't think the doctor ever really got over the fact that Andy had died after this basically minor operation. And with Andy's death, though he hadn't been treated that nicely by the city, the lights of New York were diminished.

alone

I got home and my mother was still dead. And I thought, my mother would never again tell me she thought I was terrific, we would never sit around reading books and talking about them, we would never laugh together, I would never be able to show my mom whatever it was I was working on and have her say, "I think it really starts to take off around page thirty," and I would never have her say to me again, "Look, I'm not rich, but you can always come and live here with me and it won't cost anything and we can be together."

I had waited on line with my mom when she collected unemployment in the grim offices with the steelworkers who had also been laid off back in the seventies and were waiting to collect.

We had lived in bleak apartments and trailers and we had gone to the library and gotten out armloads of books and read and read and swapped back and forth while we ate tuna fish sandwiches.

We had shopped together for clothes at the Salvation Army and then at home tried everything on, pleased with our purchases even though we had spent more than we should have, but some of the things were half off and we knew the things were nice so we had splurged. When the three of us moved in 1970 to the rabbi's apartment outside Boston, it was so my mother could be near her sister. Although her sister had found her the apartment, not too far from her large Newton Highlands home, after we moved there, my aunt did not really want anything to do with us. My mom adored her sister, though. That's why we moved there. Mom got very sick. She got sicker and sicker. She lay in bed, coughing. I was fifteen. It irritated me to have my mother lying around, so sick. She kept calling her sister, but her sister was busy. I don't know why or how her sister could have been so busy. She only lived a ten-minute drive away. Days passed. Mom wasn't getting any better. I used this situation to my advantage. I told my mother I wanted a skunk. "No!" my mom said weakly.

I didn't care. I whined, I wheedled; I was going to get me a pet skunk. I think they might have been somewhat popular at that time—they were sold, de-scented, in pet stores.

Mom got weaker and weaker. Right before I thought she was going to die, I went out on a babysitting job. The family had a pet skunk. It was not nice. I came back. "Okay, you're not going to believe this," I said. "The people I was babysitting for had a pet skunk. I don't want one now. It smelled, even though it was de-scented, and it wasn't nice."

The next day Mom finally found a doctor who would make a house call. He came over and took her to the hospital.

She was almost dead, from pneumonia.

Her sister never came around.

I don't know why some families like each other, or at least are able to put on an act.

When my mom died, my brother quickly called my aunt. My aunt was older than my mom. In thirty years of my mom's teaching at Cornell she had never been to visit her. Now she called me up. She left a message. "Sam told me that Phyllis had died. I was surprised! I remember I always found her to be a very interesting person. I remember when my mother brought her home from the hospital. I was four years old. Mother put her on the bed. I thought, Oh, that's interesting. I always found your mother to be interesting. Would you send me her books?"

Here's the thing: my aunt was eighty-nine at that time. I know, that's pretty old. Still, you'd think that by then you would know what to say, like, "I'm so sorry your mother died, my heart goes out to you!" or something like that.

My mother had always given her sister her books of poetry when they were published, but I guess she had thrown them out.

Now my mom was dead and all her older sister could say was that she had found her younger sister to be *interesting*.

My mother would never again ask me to read one of her poems she was working on; I would never be able to pick up the phone and talk to her. I would never again be able to get her advice, her reassurance, her support. I would never have a mother again.

a fine romance

You know how in those books, the middle-aged woman in search of inner peace and a new way of living moves to Bali and meets a Brazilian, like the way Diane von Furstenberg did, and falls in love and brings him home? Like the books and real life, it was hot and heavy all right. But Diane von Furstenberg dropped her hot Brazilian shortly after being on the cover of *New York* magazine, and as for those romantic popular nonfiction books, they always ended before daily routine and existence reared its head.

The contractor decided he was better off staying with his Christmas shop–owner girlfriend and helping her find lichen for her reindeer. She didn't need him to go with her to a Wild Game Dinner at a sports club. She was independently wealthy and didn't go to that kind of thing.

It wasn't until almost a week after my mom died that the contractor came over. My kid was just back from a trip with her dad, hanging around for a week before she had to go back to university. He came bristling up the drive and he saw her and said, "Willow, did you get your brakes fixed?"

That's when I remembered, he had mumbled to me at some point that Willow should get the brakes fixed on her car. But you know what? My mom had died, I wasn't thinking straight.

"No, I don't need my brakes fixed." She scowled at her mom's almost ex-boyfriend.

"Oh right!" I said. "Didn't you say you were going to get them fixed? My memory's gone. You have to keep up with this kind of stuff. You *need* to have them fixed."

"They're fine. I've driven everywhere with them."

"You have to get your brakes fixed! You're driving back to college on Sunday!" the contractor said.

"You can't drive with those bad brakes," I told her.

"I have been driving with the brakes like this for months, it's fine. If I die, I die."

"No, that is not fine! You will also maybe kill others."

That night I went to sleep happy Willow was home. It had been hard, being alone in the house with my mom just having died. Then, when Willow got back from England and New York City (that was the Tuesday after my mom died on Sunday), she went right back to work at her job as turn-down maid at the hotel in Watkins Glen from three in the afternoon until eleven at night. I didn't try to stop her. Was she supposed to sit here in the house with me while I wept? She loved being a turn-down maid. Just because I was depressed didn't mean I had to spoil the end of her summer, did it?

So she worked Wednesday and Thursday and Friday and that job was finished. She would return to college on Sunday. She got back okay on Friday. I remember, because I would wait up for her to get back from work, due to the fact that her job ended at eleven at night, in a region where deer waited on the sides of the roads until a car came by and then would spring out and try to wreck the car and kill the person.

And when she got in, that Friday night, I heard her car and I finally fell asleep.

But around 1 A.M., I woke up from a vivid dream, so real that it jolted me awake. In the dream the contractor was maybe four years old and he was just running around the room naked from the waist down, with nothing but a T-shirt on, the way little kids do when they escape from a bath before the adult has gotten a chance to re-clothe the kid. There was wall-to-wall carpeting and the contractor (he wasn't a contractor at that age) was running toward a sofa where Doug, his older brother, was sitting.

I had never met Doug, but I knew it was Doug. That's what dreams do, you know. In the dream Doug was saying to the con-tractor, "Well, hello, Lacy!" The contractor was this little boy danc-ing, floating around, from the sofa across the carpeting, like a piece of lace.

I thought, "Hello, Lacy"?

What could that possibly mean? It was peculiar. I thought, That's rubbish! Maybe the older brother was saying, "Hello, Lazy"?

But no. In the dream, he had said, quite clearly, "Hello, Lacy!"

I tossed a bit. It was very unlikely. Take these tough rednecks who were hunters and worked rough: these guys in snowplowing, construction, logging, plumbing, garbage hauling. They didn't go around calling each other "Lacy."

But, whatever. I went back to sleep.

In the morning the car fix-it shop was closed and wouldn't open all day.

I called the contractor, and he told me what parts to get, and I sent Willow with my credit card to the auto place. When she got the parts, he said, she should drive to his house. He would fix it.

A little while later she called me and said, "Mom, they have the parts I needed for my car. But I lost your credit card."

I had to give my other credit card number over the phone, but at least that worked.

Now, how could she lose my credit card between when I handed it to her, in the house, and her going to the car? That's what being a mother means. I spent two hours searching for that card and calling to cancel it and so on.

Then I went to the contractor's house. He was fixing Willow's car. She drove it around the block. There was still something wrong with it. So he worked on it some more. It was fixed, but he still wanted her to go around the block again. While we were waiting for her to come back, his phone rang and he answered it. He looked at me. He had turned white. He said, "I gotta go."

"Huh?"

"They found my brother Doug's body in the lake."

So he left. Willow came back and asked, "Where is he?" but he had gone.

Once again he quit speaking to me. I was accustomed to it. I texted him, he wouldn't text back. I called him, he didn't call back. I knew the routine: he had just done this to me when my mother died.

He did not like emotional situations or stress or pressure. Maybe he just didn't like me, I do not know.

But I kept thinking about that dream I had had. After a few days I texted his sister Suzette. I wrote, "You wouldn't know the details of this because you are younger than the contractor, so I don't know if you were even born during the time that my dream took place."

I told her about that dream, and how Doug was young and the contractor was young, and Doug called the contractor "Lacy."

"No, I don't know what you're talking about," said his sister.

I texted her, "Can you ask your father about my dream and see if he knows?"

And she told my dream to the contractor's father.

Then she texted me back. "My dad says, when the contractor was little, Doug called him Lacy."

the history of mankind

Don't get me wrong, I'm not blaming my parents.

Of course I'm blaming my parents! Just as they blamed their parents and their parents blamed their parents, this has gone on since, gosh, I don't know, early hominid? In my opinion all of humankind is one bad genetic experiment. People should not be left to their own choices propagating the human race.

But then the problem arises that even if you select the finest Nobel Prize winner and breed her to the best possible male specimen on the planet, it still isn't going to work. There's a 99.9 percent chance it's just not going to turn out well.

After college, I moved back in with my mother. Then I went back to grad school and after that, when my mother was at Princeton as an Alfred Hodder Fellow, I moved back with her again. This was 1979. I mean, my mother was brilliant. She was a poet whose manuscripts had been chosen for publication by Elizabeth Bishop, by Maxine Kumin. After Princeton, A. R. Ammons picked her to teach at Cornell. This didn't happen until she was fifty years old.

She had been a dietician, married, fired when pregnant. Then, when the kids were nine or ten, this man—her husband—was screwing everything in sight. Other women have covered this territory in other books. Now, maybe it is not so shocking. Not so horrifying. Then, just imagine the lives for women: get married and have kids.

You just couldn't envision any other life for yourself—because there wasn't any! And especially not if you came from a poor place. Of course she tried to hang on to her marriage, she was a nice Orthodox Jewish girl who had married a Jewish doctor who was . . . a scam artist, a con artist. A narcissist. At the end of the marriage, he had his secretary—with whom he was having an affair, who had divorced her husband over him—move in with us, while they were still sleeping together! There was Mom, Dad, two kids, and Dad's mistress.

Anyway, I'm backtracking. At this point, I was twenty-two, twenty-three years old.

I had a B.A. from Barnard College, cum laude, I had just gotten an M.A. on a full scholarship from Hollins, I had just been accepted to the Yale School of Drama in playwriting, and I was working on another book—my second, or third, though I was still unpublished.

But I didn't have a job. I had moved back in with Mom. I wasn't asking Dad to support me. Nevertheless, the first hate letter arrived from my father: "You are NOTHING. You will NEVER amount to anything. You are WORTHLESS." The letter was concise and to the point—it was true, I didn't have a job, I was, for the moment, back with my mom. Wanting to be a writer was, after all, a pretty stupid idea.

I was devastated. Fortunately, a week or so later, my first book was accepted, but really the damage was done; my father wasn't impressed. When he read the book (*American Dad*), after it came out, he wrote to me how I had destroyed people's lives. On the other hand, he did add how he no longer felt alone on the earth, since finally someone was writing about him.

His hate letters were so vituperative and vitriolic. He sent them to me throughout my life, at random, with arbitrary venom not directed at anything that made particular sense. He would nag and nag me: "Come visit! When will you come visit!?" It was not easy to get up there, without a car, broke, all the way from New York City. Still, like Charlie Brown, who gets the football held up in front of him only to have Lucy jerk it away at the last second, I went, year after year.

"How about in two weeks?"

"No! You can't come then. We're having people to dinner."

"In three weeks?"

"We're off to Maine."

August wasn't going to work because his in-laws were visiting for two weeks. In all the twenty-five years of the third marriage, I was never deemed worthy enough to meet Gigi's parents.

I don't know why I always went to visit after his command was issued. Once there, if I asked to use their washing machine and dryer (normally I had to take my clothes to a coin Laundromat) he would say, "Ask Gigi," and then she said, "No—it would use too much electricity."

"Would you like some vegetables from the garden to take with you?"

"No, Julian, don't give her any—there won't be enough for us." (The garden was at least a half acre.)

Nor did I ever get up quickly enough from a meal to clear the table, wash the dishes, and vacuum the floor, which always got Dad very angry.

It was long-standing. When I was eleven, I was told I couldn't attend Dad's second wedding—to Annette—because "We're going to drop acid at the ceremony. It's not appropriate for you to be there."

"But Grandma is coming!"

"Not you."

For the third wedding, he didn't invite me, he said, because "Gigi's parents are going to be there." I got it: I was the Elephant Girl.

Even when I visited on a designated date, he wouldn't speak to me, or he would scream at me.

After a visit, usually he would continue not to speak to me for months. He had descended into the black hole of rage against me. Sometimes, this would happen while I was there, for the two days he would finally allow me to visit (after begging me to come) when he decided he could, after all, squeeze me in for that weekend. I would arrive, bearing gifts I could not afford.

I would get a report months later, sometimes by hate letter, sometimes by phone, sometimes through a third party. My father and his wife (a social worker) had reached their diagnosis: I was a borderline personality.

What is borderline personality disorder? According to the National Institute of Mental Health, "Borderline personality disorder (BPD) is a serious mental illness marked by unstable moods, behavior, and relationships."

Of course, being slow-witted, it was many more years before I actually took the time to find out what a borderline personality was, and then I learned it was an asocial, amoral person, manipulative and needing to be the center of attention and so on. It didn't surprise me. When I was eight years old Dad called me manipulative: I had some bunnies and they needed a cage and Dad said he would build them a cage and then he claimed *I had manipulated him into doing it.*

Years went by. I don't know how long I lived with this knowledge and diagnosis. It turned out, people with this disorder might actually *kill* someone! Why did he want me to keep coming back! "You know," I finally said, "it always troubled me, that you and Gigi diagnosed me with this."

"What?" my dad said. "Oh, no. It wasn't you who we decided had this. It was . . . um . . . it was Veronica's sister!"

it's a man's world

Dad sent me a birthday present! I called him to say thank you. As usual, Dad started in right away about selling his property to the Audubon Society, how *maybe* there will be a tiny amount of money left for me and my brother. He wants, from the Audubon Society, a lifetime tenancy, eight to ten million, and the stipulation that, on his demise, the place will become a writers' and artists' retreat.

What kind of person doesn't leave their stuff to their kids? My brother helped him *build* his house, for crying out loud. It was the summer he was eighteen, for no pay, *of course*. The truth is that my brother was always good and earnest and sincere; he became a doctor, but my dad considers him a total failure—as he does me.

Don't ask why, but thirty years ago a couple of friends gave me a ride to Dad's. This was when *Slaves of New York* was a bestseller, but all he could say was that my short stories were "too choppy," and "Why don't you write *novels*?" We were all sitting around having dinner before my friends went on to Vermont or something, and Dad's wife said, at the table, "Tama, do you think your book was a bestseller because of your looks?"

My girlfriend let out a squawk and said, "Because of her looks? Her *looks*?" and she was cackling away and I don't know which was worse, to have Dad nodding at the thought, Yes, it certainly wasn't because her stories were any good that that book succeeded, and his wife making it clear they had figured this out, that since the book was so bad it had to have succeeded for some other reason, which was . . . my looks, which got my friend guffawing away, because obviously *that* couldn't be the reason.

I was screwed however you look at it. Of course, years later he was like, "Say, why don't you go back to writing short stories? Your stories are better than your novels."

I had gotten a break from him telling me on every phone call that he was selling his property to the Audubon Society. I kind of blotted it out when he stopped mentioning it. Maybe he found out they were only going to give him a paltry amount. But no, he was back to it. He wasn't going to leave it to his kids, and not to his granddaughter, either, although he had told me, "Now *she* is a nice kid."

Philip Roth's mother must have walked around all the time telling him how great he was. Not that Philip Roth ever had nice things to say about his mother in any book! But I figured this out because of my dad. His mother, Grandma Anne, would take people *with* him into the bathroom when he was a little kid so they could watch him whiz into the pot. She would wake him up from a sound sleep to take him in to pee, with whatever guests were around, so they could admire his micturition *and* get a glimpse of the schlong, which, rumor had it, was very large.

Then there was Wife 2 and Wife 3, and in between there were others, patients who mostly (according to Dad) came to him for past sexual traumas. Once, we—me, Mom, and my little brother— came into my dad's place, unannounced, and found him in coitus with Natasha in the master bedroom. He "dated" Violet, who, after he ended both his romance and doctor/patient relationship with her, came in and defecated on his downstairs workroom floor.

There was Emily (owned a greenhouse); and Barbara (had to get rid of her dog, a St. Bernard, to move in with him; relationship lasted only briefly); and Carole (soft sculptor); and another Barbara (had a two-year-old); and Marie-Victorine, who was living with him when he took me, Mom, and my brother to camp out in St. John, but when we got back . . . curiously, Marie-Victorine was gone! She left him for another woman, a fact that Dad later denied.

I can't even remember all of them now. There was the woman with ninety million dollars—he *hated* her because apparently she talked too much! No matter how nice and kind she was, he hated her. He was horrified that somebody could get that much money from their husband in a divorce settlement. Obviously, these were bad people.

There was, next, a very large woman who—as he said in disgust—was still married and didn't want to get divorced, but her husband didn't have sex with her. This was later in life, when Dad went on and on about how he had to take Viagra because his prostate was enlarged and how this large woman was very sexually demanding but he was finally able to get rid of her when, as he sat in a chair or bench by his swamp, the woman leapt upon him, out of pure lust, and knocked him backward, toppling him to the ground and painfully crushing him.

It was amazing. A simple walk in the woods with Dad around his estate? Women just popped out from behind the bushes, giggling, or you would come across them casually sunbathing topless atop a rocky outcropping, just out there in the middle of nowhere. I'm not making this up, it was surreal: the nervous giggles and come-hither looks—as well as the glares at me, not knowing I was his daughter and not a rival.

Shortly after he married Wife 3, Gigi, Dad decided to retire. He handed in his license to practice psychiatry, because otherwise it would have been revoked. One too many women had tried to get his license revoked before. This time, it was a high school girl who claimed he had slept with her.

Dad vehemently denied it. He said she was mentally ill. But too many women had made similar accusations in the past. So he decided the easiest thing would be to forget the whole thing and give up psychiatry. All the money his parents spent, getting him through college and through medical school and residency . . . gone. He was about fifty when he "retired."

Thankfully, Gigi was able to support him. She worked full-time, and as Dad liked to say frequently, in front of her, "Hahaha! I get to stay home and play all the time while *she* has to work!"

After she left him, Dad had no clue as to why. "Gee, Dad," I said, "maybe that wasn't the best thing to keep saying in front of her?"

"What?" said Dad. "No, no, no—she *liked* her job."

Of course she did. When Willow was, like, five years old and she wanted to water some of his plants, Dad said, "Hahaha! Isn't this great! I sit here while my granddaughter works!" and Willow immediately stopped. Even Tom Sawyer had more sense than to announce, "Hahaha! I fooled you! You're whitewashing a fence and I'm not."

So Dad not only wanted you to work, tidy, cook, and clean when you visited him, but he wanted to revel in your servitude—and to revel in his *not* doing those grim tasks.

Maybe we could just leave the work to the man my brother and I called "Dad's real son," some guy named Alan, who Dad decided to make executor of the estate after he got angry that my brother went to court and got power of attorney over his father-in-law. I didn't know who he was, exactly; I only met him once or twice. He came hanging around Dad, and Dad kind of . . . set him on the right path—although I don't know what path he was on.

Dad shared too much information. If a guy was about to come over, Dad might say, "He's in transition to being a woman! He used to be a lumberjack, and he had his Adam's apple removed. The last time he was here, he wanted to take a hot tub with me, so I could look at his new breasts—and I didn't want to, because he is NOT a pretty woman."

Okay, so these things happen to people. Still, you don't need to sneer at someone who is your friend who went through this. But it was just one more confirmation to Dad: he was better than everyone.

Maybe it's a genetic flaw, but I want to repeat all the strange facts about people. I'm a writer, maybe that's my excuse. Or it runs in the family, like my grandmother, his mom, who kept saying, "My doctor told me I have the breasts of a sixteen-year-old!" when she was about eighty. Some images, they never go away.

my little brother

In the years before my mom died, I had to move her from one nursing home to the next. I was still trying to figure out a way I could get her back home. Meanwhile, my brother's angry and accusatory e-mails grew in frequency, length, and demands. He asked over and over for all the bank statements and Mom's retirement fund statements. I tried and gave up. "When you come to visit," I said, "everything's in a box, you can go through it all and take all you want." But he never did look.

I sent him what I could. He examined all the receipts. "You used Mom's credit card at the ice cream store! You claim you were buying her an ice cream! No one spends thirty dollars on an ice cream!"

I had to submit the addendum: the thirty dollars on mom's credit card had gone to the ice cream parlor for a cake for the entire nursing home on her birthday.

I couldn't explain every detail. I couldn't keep on top of the bills, the endless paperwork that came with having Mom in a nursing home. He insisted I hand everything over to him and give him power of attorney and executorship. But Mom had told me many times, "Please don't let your brother get power of attorney! Please don't let your brother get any control! I don't want him around me."

I forget when she said this exactly. Maybe it was after Veronica told her she was an overweight hunchback. I just know my mom said she didn't want anything more to do with them. Years before, she went to a lawyer because she wanted to rewrite her will so that Sam's wife wouldn't end up with her property. But this ended up being too complicated. Eventually, after she paid the lawyer close to a thousand dollars, she gave up.

I asked Mom's accountant to send her tax returns to my brother. It took me so long just to get the info! I was trying to keep on top of my life, which just wasn't really . . . working out for me.

Sam got the tax returns and wrote back to the accountant, who contacted me. "Your brother says your mother's retirement investments are terrible. Please explain to him, I am the accountant, I'm not in charge of her investments! He didn't include a return address. Please! Your brother is very angry."

The accountant was alarmed and agitated. He was eighty years old and Mom had been going to him for thirty of them. Now I had to do damage control and soothe an octogenarian CPA.

Day after day in my mom's house I packed and tried to get rid of stuff. I also filed and put things away, like the retirement statements, which came tumbling in every day. When Sam came from Alabama—he came twice a year, for two days, to see Mom for two hours each day—I told him, "If you want the records and statements, they are in those boxes. They're all yours!"

But he didn't. Sometimes he would come up with his wife. She wouldn't come in the house, even though she had come all the way from Alabama. She waited in the car outside. I said, "Won't Veronica come in?"

"No."

They went back to Alabama and the demands and accusations started again. Finally, in May of the third year I had been looking after Mom, my brother's letters really took a turn: he said I had been committing Social Security fraud, embezzling from her estate, and about twenty thousand other things.

I was scared. I had no idea I was committing those crimes. Each month her Social Security check was deposited in her bank account, and I used that money to pay for her nursing home, then the bills were submitted to her insurance company, and so forth.

Impossibly, it got worse. More missives arrived. He had gone online, somewhere, somehow, and come up with figures for Tim's income for the past ten years, down to the last penny. He said I was very rich and that he was going to take legal action since I claimed to be broke. I had Tim's "fortune," plus, he added, "You make *tons* of money from your books."

Yes, I went to an office with Tim and signed a piece of paper once a year. No, I did not read the amounts we were paying in taxes. That wasn't on the page I signed. I did not have that kind of marriage. What Tim earned, he earned in commission—sometimes people paid promptly, sometimes not for months. I didn't know anything about it. If I asked Tim how much money there was, he said he didn't know, and I'm sure that was the truth.

If I earned money, I used it to pay bills; if I didn't have money, I asked Tim for some. It's not even that. The kid had been in private school in New York City, which cost fifty grand before taxes; there was a mortgage on the apartment, plus maintenance; Tim traveled to all the art fairs, he went out to dinner every night, he took taxis—it wasn't my business! I always thought I would be able to earn my own way in life, then I couldn't, and Tim's job ended, and . . . *there was no savings!*

My own brother doing this to me! And there was no assurance that those figures he found online for his brother-in-law's in-come were actually true. It was an invasion of everything. And so creepy! Who would spend so much time researching their sister's husband's income?

In addition to being broke and stuck, I was discouraged. Tim couldn't keep sending money because he didn't have it. And like in the movie *Groundhog Day,* I was perpetually doing one thing: cleaning out my mom's house. There were papers—student papers, graded papers, test papers. There were photographs from her parents, box after box, there were her parents' papers, my papers, my press clippings, my drafts of novels, her drafts of poems. There were closets full of old clothes, clothes she bought at the Salvation Army, my castoffs, things I bought for her.

No money had ever been put into the house and the walls were covered with mold. She always said, "I'll get it repainted when I sell the place." Meanwhile the floors were rotting, the kitchen was circa 1949, and I was living there with a kid who was going to high school and smoking pot in the room downstairs with the foul old bathtub and sink. I picked up my kid after school and took her to glass-blowing lessons, I was trying to write, but let's face it, I couldn't write. I could barely take notes.

The only thing I did that brought me any happiness was horse-back riding—and yes, I wrote a check each month on my mom's account to lease a horse. I wasn't making a salary and this was my life's sole pleasure, and not an expensive one. I continued to pay the bills, the TV, the phone, the heat—whatever, I was paying bills. When my brother's letters had started, three years before, they were merely stern, with instruction such as, "No, you can't install a walk-in bathtub for Mom. It will cost too much."

She couldn't pick up her legs to get in the tub, and she hated bathing anyway, so what was I supposed to do, wrestle her down, lift her with my superhuman strength, and throw her in the tub? I should have enjoyed those days when the misery from him was only intermittent, but I couldn't have known the accusations would escalate to big-time crimes.

I needed a lawyer.

The first one I went to had an office upstairs on the commons in Ithaca. The office was small, quaint, and charming, with wood paneling and a collection of boxes: old cigar boxes, inlaid wooden boxes, puzzle boxes—and old prints on the wall. "Sorry I'm late. I was in court." He was handsome, with a long face and a soft, bemused expression; he had a soothing aura, like Atticus Finch, the lawyer father in *To Kill a Mockingbird*. Then he looked at the letters my brother had written and he said soothingly, "It looks like you'll do serious time. Have the police been to you yet?"

"No," I said.

"Well, when they come to question you, be polite and just say, contact my lawyer, then give them my card." He handed a few to me. "Don't tell them anything—just call me right away so I'll know they are going to contact me."

The second lawyer I went to was in a big fancy corporate place, upstairs from the bank, with generic hotel/office furniture and a fluorescent-lit conference room. He had written my mother's will, and he had written the paperwork for her trust, whatever that was. When I showed him the letters my brother had written, he dropped them like they were covered in ricin. "You have committed a number of serious crimes! I can't represent you—I represent your mother. You have to find someone else."

The third lawyer was a personal friend. His offices were also on the commons—again, upstairs from a shop—but not as nice as the first lawyer's. There was gray carpeting and a vinyl couch and it wasn't charming. His company dealt with very poor criminals.

When I explained the situation and gave him my brother's letters he looked into space for a long time and said, "It's going to depend whether you're going to be prosecuted for a Class C felony, or Class D. Class C you will be doing three to seven. Class D is five to fifteen."

"But . . . I had no idea what I was doing was wrong! I was living there looking after my mom every day and I had no money to live on. I was spending money the same as I would be paying someone else to look after her."

"If you had paid someone else to look after her, that would have been okay. But you can't take money to live on."

"I didn't know!"

"That doesn't matter. Also, you had no legal right to sell your mom's house."

"She left it to me in her will. It was falling down! It was going to cost more and more money to keep it up. I couldn't live there anymore."

"You could have lived there," he said bitterly. "I have to live with my mother."

All the lawyers made it pretty clear: I was going to do time. And all three had said I'd better find a bookkeeper and get all the accounts put together. And my brother's letters continued in an endless stream. Finally I told him, "Okay, I'll divorce Tim and sell the apartment, and that way I'll have half the money from the sale."

This news seemed to placate him but he wanted me to divorce *right away* and he wanted a strict accounting *immediately*.

i get an accountant

I found a pair of women named Wanda and Dawn who had a bookkeeping firm. They took the papers and put them online in some kind of accounting program. The letters from my brother didn't stop, but at least his focus had turned on the bookkeeping company for doing a bad job. When Dawn (who owned the company) heard all the stuff from my brother and saw how he was operating, she told me to get a lawyer. I told her how my recent experiences with lawyers had gone, and she referred me to a different one.

The lawyer she knew was very nice, even though he was an hour farther away and I had to *drive*. I had to use the device that gives directions, and that thing makes me very nervous. That woman's voice got all agitated like she was going to have a nervous breakdown if I didn't turn right in three hundred yards, and I was going to have a nervous breakdown because it's hard enough to drive without this crazed woman getting frantic. I switched it to a man's voice, but forget it, he was bossy and superior and patronizing and I hated him even more. The device was technically some form of GPS, but my car was so old I had to attach the thing to the windshield and it would fly off and go dead and I was alone on the road so what was the point?

At least this lawyer didn't think I was going to do hard time. "Look," he said, "you didn't know it was wrong. It's not like this client I had, he had POA on his mom's estate and he took a million from it and he gambled the money and lost it. How much did you spend from your mom's estate?"

"I don't know," I say miserably. "It was over a three-and-a-half-year period."

"Your situation is different," he says. "It's much more like this daughter of a friend of mine: she was playing in Little League and she was a great pitcher and the night before the big game the authorities came to her and they said, 'Listen, that pitch is illegal. You can't use that pitch.' She didn't know it was an illegal pitch. That's much more your situation."

He was the fourth lawyer I had been to, and not just the only one so far who wasn't certain I was going to jail, but the only one to compare my situation to Little League, so I gave him a retainer. He urged me to get all the paperwork my brother was asking about to the bookkeepers.

I wrote check after check from my mother's accounts (on which I was a joint account holder, or the account had been left in trust for me) and called place after place on an endless search for whatever paperwork they needed. Miraculously, my brother became even more vicious. He couldn't believe the records for 2011 were not yet online! He couldn't believe I didn't have my mom's statements from John Hancock, where she had a seventeen-thousand-dollar life insurance policy! If he got any more agitated he was going to spontaneously combust, so I lived in hope.

The strange thing is that, just like with his insane knowledge of Tim's finances, it became clear that he knew where every single account of hers was, with figures down to the last penny. So why, year after year, had he kept screaming at me that he needed to know everything? "As beneficiary I am entitled to a strict accounting!"

Dude, as a human being you are entitled to shut the hell up. But what's the use? Now I'm under his thumb.

And months go by.

bookkeeping

I was scheduled to meet with the bookkeepers again so I could tell them what every single check and penny was spent on, whether it was for something personal or my mom. I was sure I didn't remember every expense from three years ago, but whatever, I'd show up and try. Then Mom died. And my brother wrote to the bookkeeper, "Where is the update! There have been no updates since June."

The bookkeeper wrote back, "We had a meeting scheduled for August. But as you may remember, your mother died. The meeting was postponed."

My brother really didn't care. I was still looking for papers. He sent me more angry e-mails. "I might have given you some extra money from Mom's estate because you looked after her. But because you were so duplicitous you will pay me back any money you took."

Further: "You were there to look after Mom in her house. BUT YOU PUT HER IN A NURSING HOME."

Didn't he understand? She was dangerous to herself and to others. The home aides had quit. The first nursing home called me at 7 A.M. the day after I took her there: "You come get your mother

NOW! We can't handle her." The second nursing home asked me to remove her by the end of the first month. She had maybe seven months at the next place, then they told me to find a higher level of care. If the nursing homes—fully staffed, fully equipped—couldn't handle her, how could I have done so? But my brother made me feel terrible that I had not taken care of Mom at home.

That person in the home, though, that was not my mom. My mom was dead, but she had left a long time ago. It was October and I was alone on this planet. I went to Dawn the bookkeeper. "As soon as we get these papers from your mom's retirement plan"—printouts of three and a half years of every buy, sell, and trade she made—"we can get this into the system and almost everything will be done. Look how close we are to finishing this job! It looks like based on this information, we are getting close to what you spent over the three and a half years."

Dawn was so nice and sympathetic to my plight. That's what it was, a plight. I just couldn't believe I had made this great and supportive new friend; I wanted to hang out with her. "And soon your bro will leave you alone . . . although surely you are entitled to some compensation for spending all your time looking after your mother."

"I wasn't doing it for compensation. If I had the income I wouldn't have spent her money—but I had to live. And . . ." I showed her the e-mail from my brother where he said he would not let me take reimbursement for my time or work. She shook her head.

"I will be away for ten days, but Wanda will work on it, and when I get back, we'll have one more meeting and I think it will be all done! So, keep the faith! By the way, while I'm away—don't tell Wanda *anything*. She is just my intern. I'm trying her out." She handed me an invoice. I wrote her a check in her office.

"Thank you, Dawn. Thank you for your kindness and sympathy and help. I would be so lost without you and your kind words."

A week later, I was on my way out of town; a friend had invited me to Florida. I hadn't been anywhere in almost two years, and then it was only for two days. I had to have a vacation. I was totally alone.

I had a layover in Philadelphia, where I discovered the following e-mail:

Tama,

Your check bounced. I am out of the country on vacation and I need for you to get Wanda $661.55 in cash as soon as possible. The fact that this has happened is not sitting well with me. You have to give the cash to Wanda TODAY.

Kindly text me to let me know that you have received this email.

You have placed me in a very difficult position financially and I do not appreciate it at all. When I return we can talk about the future of our working relationship.

Thank you for your prompt response to this email.

What? I was so embarrassed and upset! "I am in the airport," I e-mailed her immediately, apologizing. "I truly don't know how this happened—there is plenty of money in that account." I called the bank and they said, "Your name is not on the accounts. You only had POA, which stopped as soon as your mother died."

This was a different story than what I'd been told. I apologized to Dawn, over and over, but her angry e-mails continued—just like my brother's!

It turned out that the account on which I had written the check not only had the money in it (visible to Dawn) but also had—as I had thought—been left in trust for me. Only the bank had lost the card stating this.

Now I had to start from scratch. It was mid-November, pitch dark at 5 P.M. It was cold and already there were snow flurries. Hunting season would start soon.

When I took a look at the work Dawn had done, what had been recorded on the QuickBooks accounting program—all of it was incorrect! She'd written down vast amounts of money that weren't there, that had never been there. She'd simply made up numbers; it was completely wrong.

At night the coyotes howled and screamed all night, right outside my door. And in the day my brother emitted via e-mail his punitive cries—only his were filled with hate and vitriol. He decided to take me to court. I'm still waiting for the trial. It's coming up soon. My brother's retired now. He has five million in the bank, plus property. I've got a lawsuit in a month—he's trying to sue me because my mother left me two small accounts he wants half of. Me, the life of a writer? I'm broke.

no conclusion

What happens? What happened.
   Here I am, eight years old, they hauled me out of second or third grade at Smith Day School to model for the alumni magazine.

No kidding. And life, too. That happens.

Just before Christmas of 1986, Andy said he had a Christmas present for me that he would give me when he got back from Milan. But then he died. Twenty-nine years later, in 2015, the portrait of me appeared in the *New York Times*. It was found in his house, following his death, but had not yet been stitched together. I never did receive it.

I wanted to include it because (a) I appear deranged and have only one eye, (b) it represents a major change and breakthrough in Andy's art, and (c) I am and will be the only person to have a portrait done by Andy and *also* appear in a Spider-Man comic. This, to me, is proof of my existence. But I couldn't. Reprint rights were expensive. Here is my attempt at a similar portrait.

this box deliberately
left empty

This is not a portrait of Tama Janowitz by Andy Warhol.

This is a self-portrait drawn by Tama Janowitz.

I'm still with the contractor and am waiting for my trial. I am writing. I am riding my horse. Most of the past is a blur because only the present exists. But there are still a few things that make me smile when I reflect back. Like, one time I got a call, back in New York City. A man said, "Hi, Tama. I am calling to ask if you would appear on a talk show with Peter Parker—he's just published a new book of photographs."

"Well, no," I said. I mean, I was thinking, why would I go on a talk show to promote someone else's book? I have enough trouble promoting my own, and I get very nervous going on talk shows. "He's booked on a talk show and he can't promote his own work, himself?"

"You don't understand," the man said. "You'd be with Peter Parker in a *comic book*. Peter Parker is Spider-Man's alias!"

"Are you serious!?" I said. "Of course I would appear in a comic book! I'd be totally thrilled!"

That's how I ended up in a Spider-Man comic.

postscript

Finally I get to go to the Snake Charmers Lounge, the bleak-looking "gentleman's club" on the tourist wine trail road, near the Christmas shop and the Glen. In summer the road is always busy. But in winter, which lasts for around nine months of the year, almost everything shuts down, except for this lounge. According to the contractor, the legal (and illegal) Mexican workers from the dairy farms need someplace to go, and they're known to spend entire paychecks on lap dances.

I've been waiting for this moment, but I was always too much of a wuss to go there on my own. The construction worker takes me. He pays admission to a grayish figure at the end of a bar—it costs something like ten dollars each—and we get soda (there's no alcohol in the place). There aren't really any customers, either, apart from us. There's a big table surrounded by bar stools and a long, glistening table with one pole, and in the corner of the room are four or five bored girls in bikini tops and panties tossing their manes and stomping their high-heeled hooves. He gives me a stack of singles. Now a girl comes out from behind a doorway and gets on the table. First she cleans the pole with some presumably antibacterial wipe and fairly promptly takes off her clothes—except for her high heels—then writhes, undulates, and performs various contortions, stopping in front of us. The construction worker tucks a dollar in her garter and she places his head between her breasts. Her dance is over. "That's one of the owner's daughters," he tells me.

"Who's the owner?" I say. "That guy who you paid at the door?"

"Yes."

A man is sitting across from us now, and another girl comes out and wipes off the pole. The man has a very appreciative expression, and as she spreads her legs, allowing him a look at her vagina, he gives her a dollar. This one is even more agile and is able to spin on the pole upside down and so forth. "That's another of the owner's daughters," he says. They have very nice bodies and dance without any sensuality whatsoever. I can't tell how old they are.

"The place is empty," I say.

"Oh, it will get crowded."

But it never does.

Each girl wipes off the pole. I can't tell if it's to get rid of the previous dancer's perspiration or if it's because each is pathologically afraid of obtaining a disease. The whole place reeks, smelling of marijuana and the kind of disinfectant that haunts you forever after you use the toilet on the bus or train. One girl is wearing striped thigh-high stockings and sleeves and platform sandals in bright clown colors, and she waves her breasts at us, bending low. "Ooh, what a cute outfit!" I say, even though that doesn't exactly seem like the right comment to make. "Where did you find matching shoes!"

Now a young girl comes out, and she doesn't *appear* to be any older than fourteen. She has to be coached by another dancer, who sits in the corner nearby, gesticulating to the girl how to move and what to do. This girl seems very nervous, unlike the owner's daughters. I'm thinking, why was I so upset when my dad wanted me to enter a wet T-shirt contest? I am just so old-fashioned, right? A strong skunky odor wafts out from the side room from which the girls emerged. I guess there's no alcohol in this place but these girls smoke plenty of pot, no doubt with their dad.

Such sad parents my daughter has, right? With her own father telling her grandfather not to get his granddaughter high and a mother who spent a lifetime trying to discourage her daughter from getting a job as a topless dancer as a career choice, and advising her not to get any tattoos. The first semester that kid was at college, the university sent out a letter at Thanksgiving warning parents not to be alarmed if their child came home with a tattoo, that it was perfectly normal. Only it was too late.

Now another girl comes out, I don't know if she is yet another of the owner's daughters or what. First she splays herself in front of the construction worker, and then, coming to me, begins to nuzzle me on the side of my face, reeking of dirty hair and that skunky smell. I want to shove her off me! Quickly I give her a dollar. How much will I have to pay to keep her away from me? If she puts one hand on me, I think, I'm going to start screaming and I won't stop. Any hope or aspiration I had of becoming a lesbian is now ended forever. My life would have been better, possibly easier, had I been gay but now I see there is truly no hope.

My contact lenses are bothering me and I should have known not to wear long underwear to this venue. It's freezing outside, there's a chance of snow, but what kind of idiot wears long underwear to a nude club? Finally we get up to leave. I take a deep breath, glad of fresh air, only . . . the smell is worse than inside. All that time indoors, it was nothing as strong as it is out here. As we get closer to the car—the side the dressing, or undressing, room was on—the odor becomes more ferocious. It really *is* a skunk! Some skunk must have pooted right under the side of the building.

Is there a moral to any of this?

None that I can think of.

Fiction has morals; fiction has a point.

Life? I guess not.

There are always two sides to aisle 11.

And sometimes, not always, aisle 12 is nearby.

acknowledgments

With much thanks and appreciation for my friends, some of whom
are also friend/agent, friend/editor, friend/publicist, friend/teacher,
friend/support—in various combinations—all of whom have saved
me in one way or another:

Christopher Schelling, Carrie Thornton, Matthew Daddona,
Joseph Papa, Greg Villepique.

Stasia Newell, Tim Dunlap, Tara Bricker, Sue Martin, Kristine
Shaw, Lyn Gerry, Cat Rossiter, Lindy Feigenbaum, Debbie
Schmitz, Diane Shetler, Susan Ward, Mark Ramos, Joe Chicone,
Anne Cridler, Annie Hauff Madison, Mark Raymond.

Jo Hunt, Mary Ott, Peter Baker, Carol Alexander, Missy
Blauvelt, Tom Bell, Millie Nash, Cathy Carlson—there when I
needed you.

To those who were with me when I was told my mom had died:
Sue Laughlin, April Borden, Sylvia Laughlin. So compassionate,
kind, and supportive.

Jill Abrams!

Sally Judd, Paige Powell, Brian Dannelly, Michael Urban,
Glenn Albin, Barton G. Weiss, Nick Fox, Fay Weldon, James
Ivory, Tim Hunt—rescuers all of you—and last, but numero uno,
Willow Hunt.

Special thanks to the New York Foundation for the Arts for their
aid—financial and psychological—at a crucial moment in my life.

about the author

TAMA JANOWITZ has published eleven books, which have been translated into twenty-two languages and made into several films. She lives in upstate New York with her dog, Zizou Zidane, now that the other seven have expired, and her quarter horse mare, Fox, with whom she studies under Stasia Newell.